D1005876

MELANCHOLY
ACCIDENTS

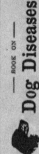

MELANCHOLY
ACCIDENTS

THREE CENTURIES OF STRAY BULLETS AND BAD LUCK

PETER MANSEAU

MELVILLE HOUSE
BROOKLYN • LONDON

MELANCHOLY ACCIDENTS

First Melville House Printing: March 2016

Melville House Publishing   8 Blackstock Mews
            46 John Street   and   Islington
        Brooklyn, NY 11201   London N4 2BT

mhpbooks.com   facebook.com/mhpbooks   @melvillehouse

Library of Congress Cataloging-in-Publication Data
Names: Manseau, Peter, author.
Title: Melancholy accidents / Peter Manseau.
Description: 1st ed. | Brooklyn : Melville House, 2016.
Identifiers: LCCN 2015049050| ISBN 9781612195063
    (hardback) | ISBN 9781612195070 (ebook) | ISBN
    9781612195063 (ebook)
Subjects: LCSH: Firearms accidents—United States—Case
    studies. | BISAC: TRUE CRIME / General. | HISTORY /
    United States / 19th Century. | SOCIAL SCIENCE / Violence
    in Society.
Classification: LCC RA772.F57 M36 2016 | DDC 363.33—dc23
LC record available at http://lccn.loc.gov/2015049050

Design by Marina Drukman

Printed in the United States of America
10 9 8 7 6 5 4 3 2 1

People shoot,
but it's God who delivers the bullet.

—SVETLANA ALEKSIEVICH

23724

GUN POWDER

Quadrille Militaire

par

CAMILLE SCHUBERT.

Author of the celebrated Mardi Gras Quadrille

NEW YORK.

Published by Wᴹ. A. POND & Cº 547 Broadway.

BOSTON.	MONTREAL.	PITTSBURGH.
O. DITSON & Cº	BOUCHER & MANSEAU.	H. KLEBER & BRO.
CHICAGO,		MILWAUKEE.
ROOT & CADY.		H.N.HEMPSTED

AMERICAN DANSE MACABRE

JUST SHORT OF THE MUZZLE of the upturned pistol that is the state of Idaho, Kootenai County is home to an adult population of around 100,000, and nearly 20,000 concealed–carry gun permits. Every year, county officials process so many new requests from citizens hoping to wear firearms hidden under jackets, slung on their hips, or strapped to their ankles, that you might think this picturesque community of mountains, lakes, and backcountry was a lawless wasteland, rather than a popular destination for outdoor sports enthusiasts. Over the past decade, the number of annual concealed–carry permit applications has increased tenfold, from fewer than 300 in 2007 to more than 3,000 in 2015. The sheriff's office has limited the number of hours its lobby is open for other business. The paperwork involved in arming the public simply takes up too much time.

Few Kootenai residents would want it any other way. Even the County Commissioner has a concealed-weapons permit. He wears his holstered sidearm during town meetings, because, he once explained, "You just never know when something is going to happen."

A twenty-nine-year-old mother spending the holidays in the county in 2014 must have felt similarly. As she and her two-year-old son walked the aisles of the Walmart Supercenter a few miles west of Coeur d'Alene National Forest just before New Year's Eve, she kept her legally concealed 9mm Smith and Wesson semiautomatic in a purse designed for that purpose, within a zippered pocket on the side of a leather shoulder bag almost indistinguishable from many available in the women's accessories section of the store.

A Christmas gift from her husband, the concealed-carry purse was a $100 "urban shoulder bag," made by an Illinois company called Gun Tote'n Mamas. According to the manufacturer's site, the bag can hold a weapon ranging in size from a snub-nosed revolver to a 1911 Commander, along with a water bottle or book, maps, wallet, and "munchies." Beneath the front flap, a six-pocket organizer provides ample room for "pens, papers, cell phone, keys, loose change, iPOD, BlackBerry, etc." A loaded handgun, in other words, was just one more tool for the modern mom on the go.

As a Gun Tote'n Mamas slogan put it, to be armed and fashionable allowed women to "Take control in style." And not to worry if your new handbag's leather seemed a bit stiff; it would "become butter soft within weeks of use."

This particular gun purse never had that chance. As mother and child made their way through Walmart, the toddler unzipped the gun pocket and reached inside. He drew the 9mm out of its Velcroed holster, pointed it up from his seat in the shopping cart, and fired at his mother from point-blank range.

Speaking soon after, local law enforcement expressed sympathy, but stopped short of surprise. "It's pretty common around here," a lieutenant at the sheriff's office said. "A lot of people carry loaded guns."

Comments from the dead woman's family likewise lent the shooting an air of inevitability. They lived their lives around weapons, the mother's loved ones explained. They were veterans of rifle clubs and hunting trips, so blasts like those that rang through the supercenter on a Tuesday morning were not usually cause for alarm; they echoed naturally through their days.

"We're gun people," her father-in-law said.

Though it was just one of the more than 1,500 accidental gun deaths to occur in America that year, the December 2014 incident at the Kootenai County Walmart instantly received international attention. Reports in the United Kingdom highlighted Idaho state legislation that expanded areas where concealed weapons would be allowed. In France, journalists reminded readers of the nearly 300 million guns in the United States. An Australian columnist noted that such numbers make gun accidents common, even though adult victims of mishaps involving toddlers remained rare. "Normally when they handle a gun," he wrote, "very young children kill themselves or other children."

Children killing adults with guns is a statistical subset small and sorrowful enough that it always receives at least local press coverage. Just three weeks earlier, an Oklahoma three-year-old had killed his mother while she changed his infant sister's diaper. And a few months before that, a nine-year-old in Arizona had killed her shooting-range instructor with an Uzi.

But something about the Idaho Walmart shooting seemed to cry out for telling and retelling, around the world and across all media. What made this story so compelling? Was it its setting, within the national ritual of the post-holiday shopping trip? Or perhaps it was the almost universal image at its core: the distracted mother hunting for deals as a curious child digs through her purse. "The details," as *The New York Times* noted, "are shatteringly ordinary." Each of them—the scene, the characters, and the perfect storm of bad judgment and misfortune—combined to give even the most basic reporting the narrative power of a carefully crafted short story.

Though the facts of the shooting were recounted with an urgency typical of the Internet age, they added up to something more haunting and elusive than we jaded consumers of twenty-four-hour news usually encounter. Here was a memento mori peculiar to our culture; a sudden recognition that guns now move through the American landscape with such ubiquity that even a family stroll through Walmart can lead to a game of Russian roulette. The story suggested that the question we collectively face is not *if* the guns all around us will fire, but *when*.

In the days following the Kootenai County tragedy, the hashtag #IdahoWalmart lit up social media. With Facebook, Instagram, and especially Twitter having become the primary means by which stories of unfortunate events are shared, lamented, and disputed, tweets and status updates about the store, the state, and the weapon hit the same sad notes for weeks. As such things do, however, this singular shooting occupied the public's outrage and imagination for a short time, only to be replaced by another.

Yet the hunger for such stories remains, as does our fascination with them. #IdahoWalmart will be a distant memory by the time these words are published, but the dark shadow that guns cast on American culture will undoubtedly endure in other digital forms. When future historians sift through the collection of several hundred billion tweets Twitter has agreed to archive at the Library of Congress, scholars studying life and death in the early-twenty-first-century United States may pay particular attention to one eight-character chain among the endless online traces that will likely survive us all: #GunFail. Used most effectively by David Waldman of the website *Daily Kos*, the Twitter hashtag identifying news items related to gun mishaps has, for several years now, provided a depressingly clear view of the many ways we find to accidentally shoot ourselves. Cleaning guns, dropping guns, "overhandling" guns, allowing guns anywhere near children or dogs—all of these occasionally lethal activities add an often over-looked dimension to the question of whether it is guns that kill people or people who kill people: while people who kill people with guns often don't mean to, guns are so good at it that people sometimes don't even have to try.

Like much of the current debate concerning the easy availability of firearms in this country, #GunFail gath-ered steam after the murder of twenty first-graders and six adults in Newtown, Connecticut, on December 14, 2012. The kinds of deaths and injuries the hashtag chronicles, however, will be mostly unaffected by the efforts to expand gun control born of that massacre. In the months following Newtown, a ban on high-capacity magazines would not have helped the three-year-old shot by his stepfather with a small caliber rifle in North Carolina. Nor would closing the gun-show loophole have saved the four-year-old who shot and killed himself with a stolen gun in Texas. Nor would more extensive background checks have protected the deputy sheriff's child who did the same in Michigan. Nothing short of transforming a culture that finds walking armed through Walmart reasonable would have saved the mother killed by her toddler in Idaho. There are certain categories of senseless tragedy we will simply continue to choose to live with.

The power of #GunFail (and, when its victims are not mothers or children, its occasional pitch-black humor) is that it is an ongoing concern: today or tomorrow, as sure as a cartoon time bomb, there is bound to be another bang. Yet its haunting quality is not merely a matter of sad predictability—of fatal accidents that occur daily and will inevitably stretch far into the future. It's also about our collective past. Because after all, we have been failing with guns for centuries. Indeed, if we could somehow hashtag history, a narrative would emerge of a nation that fancies itself created and sustained by guns, yet remains resigned to being culled by them with unnerving frequency.

Most accidental gun deaths come and go with few tears beyond those shed by the next of kin. For those who merely read about them, they become either cautionary tales of innocents in the wrong place at the wrong time (*what a pity!*), or morality plays depicting the limitless stupidity of strangers (*what a moron!*). They are parables of a sort, and from the beginning they have often been framed in religious terms.

The first American #GunFail on record seems to have occurred not long after Governor John Winthrop dreamed of establishing a "City upon a Hill" in the Massachusetts Bay Colony. By the end of its first decade, Boston's population was growing quickly, and on any given day, the sight of multiple ships carrying new settlers from England wasn't uncommon. When one of these vessels had trouble finding a place to anchor, a gunner would fire a shot meant to land harmlessly in the water—the colonial equivalent of air traffic control.

Such was the case when three ships arrived from Ipswich in mid-June 1637 with 360 passengers. The first two ships had found their anchorages without difficulty, but the third failed to go where it was directed, and so a shot was fired to guide it to a spot near Castle Island.

Gunpowder is an unpredictable substance, however. "The powder in the touchhole being wet," Winthrop noted in his journal, "and the ship having fresh way with wind and tide, the shot took place in the shrouds and killed a passenger." The gunner had fired through the rigging and hit one of the hopeful new colonists—"an honest man," who had survived the ocean passage only to be shot dead upon arrival.

The next day the governor and magistrates rowed out to view the body and determine how this tragedy had occurred. "Hearing all the evidence," Winthrop wrote, they "found that he came to his death by the providence of God."

The #GunFails of our forebears were often called "melancholy accidents." Inadvertent suicides and other firearm-induced injuries to self and others were so frequent in early America that regular listings of these melancholy accidents could be found in newspapers across the colonies and the early republic throughout the eighteenth and nineteenth centuries. Though these accident reports also took note of drownings, horse tramplings, and steamship explosions, guns provided their assemblers with the most pathos per column inch:

A melancholy accident happened at Roxbury on Monday last, two young men diverting themselves with the military Exercise, when one of them gave the Word of Command to Fire! The other instantly discharged his piece, not knowing it was loaded, and the ball entered the head of his Companion, Mr. Henry Wilson, Baker, 22, and killed him on the spot. (*Boston Evening-Post*, September 19, 1774)

A melancholy accident happened on Monday last at White's Hotel, in Falmouth; a sea-faring lad, who had been in the house a few weeks, was in the kitchen with the servant-girl, where a musket had lain for several months, and no person, from its being so foul and rusty, ever knew that it was loaded; the boy, in exercising the gun, placed it close to the girl's head, when it immediately went off; the contents of which were lodged in the poor creature's head; she instantly expired. (*The Pennsylvania Packet*, April 25, 1789)

Melancholy Accident—As Nathaniel Ellicott Force was in the act of cocking and raising a gun, it unexpectedly discharged its load, the butt end giving him a violent blow in the bowels. The gun had been heavily loaded, with nearly double the usual proportion of shot, for the purpose of shooting on the wing. Medical assistance was immediately obtained, but proved to no avail. He lived about twenty-four hours after the accident occurred in extreme suffering. (*The New York American*, July 8, 1831)

Varied as the circumstances of these deaths were, such "melancholy accidents" were regarded much like the Massachusetts Bay gunner's deadly misfire: acts occurring by the "providence of God"—unfortunate, perhaps, but largely unavoidable. Guns were as much a part of American life as the lake in which you might drown, or the draft horse that might run you over if you got in his way.

Stretching through the centuries in which the United States was born and developed, these early reports of rampant firearm mishaps provide us now with an achingly personal view into the lives of those outside history's spotlight, whose experiences—frequently violent, sorrowful, and terrifying—nonetheless helped shape the soul of the nation. To judge not only by the content of the reports but by the fact that they were popular enough that they continued in much the same form for a dozen generations, the people who read them not only lived by the gun, but were apparently fascinated by the ever-present possibility that they would die by it.

While at times recording little more than the names of those involved, the stories—under the headlines "Melancholy Accident" or "Accidental Shooting" (and sometimes simply "Distressing")—more often took the form of gem-like narratives that perfectly captured painful moments in excruciating and efficient detail. Taken together, they might be seen as a forgotten mode of American storytelling. Though we often associate accounts of life in the colonies or on the frontier with the legends of Washington Irving or the tall tales of the West, the harsh reality of the times can be better seen in reports whose clinical attention to injuries both physical and emotional make them seem torn from the pages of the pulpiest hard-boiled noir.

As in crime fiction, there is a certain sameness to many melancholy accidents. In the florid style of the day, a gunshot not only kills a man but often "puts a period to his existence." Widows tend to be "disconsolate"; the children of the dead are usually "numerous"; when one brother guns down another during a hunting expedition, it must be noted that they "had always lived in the greatest harmony together," or else suspicious readers might assume Cain and Abel had settled their score with duck shot.

Each accident is as unique as the life that preceded it, yet in their accumulated telling they are reduced to tropes. In this, there is perhaps a similarity between melancholy accidents and another long-ago attempt to understand both the individual and the universal nature of death.

In the medieval artistic genre known as the Danse Macabre, a group of skeletons would visit people from all stages and stations of life—women, men, and children; paupers, popes, and kings. In these depictions, the skeletons would lead one and all in a jig whose allegorical implication was clear: everyone was equal—inevitably—when it came to the ends they would meet. No matter one's position in life, to death all are invited. As Goethe imagined the moment when the formerly living take up the dance that recognizes them as equals at last: "In haste for the sport, soon their ankles they twitch... The young and the old, and the poor, and the rich."

Though the Danse Macabre tableaux were concerned with the universal, they grew out of a particular moment: when the bubonic plague—also known as the Black Death—killed more than 100 million people throughout Europe and Asia. The numbers of fatalities from plague and firearm mishaps are nowhere near equivalent, of course, but the preoccupation reflected in the melancholy accident reports suggests a similar attempt to contend with a ubiquitous threat. Plagues may have killed more people than guns throughout history, so far, but guns have long occupied a larger part of our collective imagination, and the fear that they may be as difficult to avoid as the most virulent contagions was at least part of the motive of those who published reports of their failure and misuse. "The instruments of destruction and death are around us wherever we go," one 1837 accident collector wrote.

If indeed melancholy accidents were once our American Danse Macabre, it is worth noting that the music plays on, even as the name of the tune has changed.

"They died by the hundreds both day and night," a fourteenth-century chronicler of the plague recalled, "and all were thrown in ditches and covered over with earth. And as soon as those ditches were filled more were dug. I buried my five children with my own hands."

This is the way we bury our children now: "A three-year-old boy is playing with a gun and shoots himself in the face," *The Washington Post*'s Mark Berman recounted in 2014. "A four-year-old girl discovers a gun and shoots her four-year-old cousin, killing him. A three-year-old boy shoots himself in the head. A five-year-old accidentally shoots a three-year-old girl. A five-year-old boy accidentally shoots and kills himself. A four-year-old boy accidentally shoots himself. A two-year-old boy shoots and kills his eleven-year-old sister. It goes on like this, story after story . . ."

There were so many to bury, the plague chronicler wrote, that the death bell did not sound. Only the echo of each loss remained.

•

Then, as now, we are but momentarily moved by unintentional death by bullet—moved, but usually not moved enough to tighten gun-control laws. Throughout U.S. history, inadvertent injuries by firearms have vastly outnumbered either mass shootings or attempted assassinations, yet it has mainly been these latter two ways of being killed by guns that have led to attempts to limit their availability.

The first such effort, the so-called "Pistol-Totin' Bill" was championed for years, beginning in 1915, by Tennessee's Senator John Knight Shields. Despite widespread concerns over rising crime rates, Shields's various bills did not receive consideration until another senator—Charles Henderson of Nevada—was shot by a disgruntled constituent in the Russell Office Building in 1921. "The recent shooting of former Senator Henderson," one contemporary account wryly notes, "served to focus the attention of the representatives and senators on the gun carrying habit, which is probably as widespread in the nation's capital as in any city in the country."

In his 1921 bill, Shields hoped to restrict interstate commerce in pistols and other small firearms, with the aim of making them so difficult to transport for sale that manufacturers would discontinue them of their own accord. Facing expected opposition from these same manufacturers, as well as from the congressmen from gun-manufacturing states, this effort did not survive.

Just as Shields's bill—doomed by the competing interests of his colleagues—was concerned with a particular type of weapon, the next concerted effort was directed at those used by the criminals who dominated the headlines of the following decade. The National Fire Arms Act of 1934 restricted the guns made famous by gangsters (and, perhaps as importantly, gangster movies): tommy guns and sawed-off shotguns. As in the current discussion of what makes an assault rifle an assault rifle, size mattered: though a "shotgun having a barrel of less than eighteen inches in length" was no more lethal than its longer brethren, the law located their greatest threat in their ability to be concealed, and thus the terror that there might be guns all around you, anywhere and anytime.

This fear of the ubiquitous gun was linked, predictably, to concern over who might have them. Even Senator Shields, pioneer of gun control, had worried most of all about those easy-to-conceal pistols getting into the hands of the wrong shade. "Can not we, the dominant race," he asked, "upon whom depends the enforcement of the law, so enforce the law that we will prevent the colored people from preying upon each other?"

The other prevailing concern—which came too late to save a president—was with how guns were obtained. After it was discovered that Lee Harvey Oswald had purchased his Italian rifle and scope by mail (for less than twenty dollars), the prohibition of mail-order weapons was hastily added to a gun bill then moving through the senate. This and similar efforts would not succeed until five years and two assassinations later, when Lyndon Johnson addressed Congress twice on the subject. "Weapons of destruction can be purchased by mail as easily as baskets of fruit or cartons of cigarettes," Johnson said. "We must eliminate the dangers of mail–order murder."

Johnson, perhaps our most gun–haunted president, lamented that in the year that saw the murders of Robert Kennedy and Martin Luther King Jr., 2 million guns had been sold in the United States. "Far too many," he said, "were bought by the demented, the deranged, the hardened criminal and the convict, the addict, and the alcoholic. We cannot expect these irresponsible people to be prudent in their protection of us, but we can expect the Congress to protect us from them." Heeding his call, when Congress passed the Gun Control Act in October 1968, the law identified classes of people prohibited from buying weapons.

Yet neither this prohibition, nor whatever comes of contemporary hopes to amend the nation's gun laws, will have ultimately done much to solve the most enduring and irrevocable risk associated with the bearing of arms. The writers of accident reports seem to have known how little could truly be done to be made safe around objects designed to do harm. While calls to take care with weapons are common ("This melancholy Accident," the *Maryland Gazette* wrote in 1760, "will be a Caution against trusting loaded Arms with Children"), the closest anyone comes to a policy proposal appears in an 1899 report included here, in which it is wondered if hunters might find a color to wear that would alert their companions that they were not in fact game. It took several decades for "red clothing" laws to spread across the country. When they did, deaths by accidental shooting dropped precipitously, but injuries by misfire, mishandling, and sheer dumb luck continued, often with fatal results. Long before #GunFail, the faded headstones of melancholy accident victims might have reminded us that the basic fact of life with guns was as true yesterday as it will be tomorrow: guns don't always do what we want them to.

It perhaps goes without saying that the common element found in all eighteenth-, nineteenth-, and twentieth-century accounts of gun accidents is violence: the penetration of bodies by metal propelled with fire. As often as the outcome of such violence was death, however, death is rarely the primary subject of the reports themselves. They are, on the contrary, concerned most of all with the living, and with the precarious hold the living have on the world. Their overall mood is one of resignation, a sense that not only were those who suffered death by bullet destined to do so, but that even surviving bystanders will spend their remaining days forever within range of similar ends.

The reports have other things in common, as well. To begin with, the majority of gun accidents collected in the press were family affairs. Fathers shoot daughters, mothers shoot sons, husbands shoot wives and, perhaps most frequently, brothers shoot sisters. Reports of the latter often strike notes of sibling mischief gone awry: younger brothers point rifles at older sisters, hoping for a laugh or a squeal. Then comes the discharge, and the game is done. In many cases, the narratives conclude with a sense that the family members of those killed or gravely wounded are left to contend with a grief that cannot be contained by a newspaper's column inches.

A shadow of abuse lingers over some of the tales; hints that not all accidents are equally accidental. Racial tensions in particular are at times laid bare. An 1867 report makes reference to Petroleum V. Nasby, the Confederate persona created by New York journalist David Ross Locke, to tell the story of a white man who unintentionally injured his brother while "engaged in the Nasbylike pastime of shooting a negro." Only occasionally are arrests made.

Given a somewhat limited range of dramatis personae (in most reports the reader meets only the shooter and the shot), the dozens of anonymous writers of melancholy accidents were also naturally drawn to the same themes. Many reports, for example, took a remarkably similar interest in trajectory—in the paths traveled by projectiles before and after they intersected with human lives. A writer in 1801 described a single shot that passed through a man's hand, then his wrist, then his shoulder, climbing his arm like a snake coiling around its prey. A writer in 1838 took care to note how a charge entered a boy's head on the left side "a little in front of the ear," before passing out the back of his head and continuing on its course. Seventeen years later, another writer described a shot stitching through a crowd like a needle drawing separate scraps of fabric together into a quilt: on its way toward the woman it killed, it passed "through the skirts of a young man's coat standing near," and then "tore the dress of a lady who was standing behind."

Mapping the progress of bullets through space and flesh, accident report writers at times lent them the heft and gravity of celestial spheres, as if the guns and their victims were simply objects in ineluctable orbit, powerless to avoid collision. If "heaven sends misfortune," a New York accident report from 1803 asks, "why should we repine?" Such a question is not so far from Job's "though he slay me, I will trust him yet"—uttered as God bore down on his unflaggingly pious servant with suffering sufficient to make even the pious challenge faith and welcome death—but the compilers of melancholy accidents were, for the most part, not particularly devout. Though they may often read like parables, rare is the accident report that finds solace in heavenly hopes.

I first stumbled upon much of the material assembled here while researching a book about religion in American history. Reading through thousands of pages of newspapers from the colonial period and the early republic, I was looking for discussions of belief, and frequently found descriptions of mayhem instead. Guns and faith are often entwined in the narrative of the nation's history, but it is not always in ways we might expect.

Garry Wills recently proposed that the gun itself functions as a god within American culture, that it is an unquestionable deity that demands supplication from all who behold it. "The gun is not a mere tool, a bit of technology, a political issue, a point of debate," Wills wrote in the aftermath of the Sandy Hook massacre. "It is an object of reverence. Devotion to it precludes interruption with the sacrifices it entails. Like most gods, it does what it will, and cannot be questioned. Its acolytes think it is capable only of good things. It guarantees life and safety and freedom. It even guarantees law. Law grows from it. Then how can law question it?"

True as this might seem when seen through the lens of a political climate in which the will of the National Rifle Association seems inscribed in tablets given from on high, the accident reports collected here paint a slightly different picture. Whatever might be said of the totems they have become, guns in American history were not seen as agents of an angry deity to be appeased, but rather—and perhaps more frighteningly—they presented to a largely religious nation blasphemous evidence of divine indifference. As one philosophical collector of accident reports in the 1780s declared upon considering how often his own life had been threatened by guns and their misuse, "it is by *accident* that we yet live." John Winthrop saw "divine providence" in gun powder's destructive power; others saw the opposite.

The accident reports gathered on the pages following were written across three centuries, from 1739 to 1916. They were published in dozens of newspapers in the English colonies and throughout the young United States. Early on, mishaps from the mother country were published nearly as often as homegrown catastrophes. As the nation grew, so too did the purview of the anonymous editors who collected them. Detailed accounts of melancholy accidents moved steadily westward with the frontier and arrived in California with the Gold Rush. While primarily seen as matters of local concern, some accidents were regarded as so melancholy that they should be shared across the vast distances of a country that seemed to know no boundaries and yet could never escape the gun. Distributed far and wide, they became a dark stitch within the narrative that bound the nation together: From New England to the Carolinas, hunting partners filled each other with lead that didn't know north from south. From New York to Mississippi, children made playthings of weapons with common results. From coast to coast, even the most happily married husbands and wives frequently found themselves separated by a shotgun blast.

To read these reports now is to bridge a gap not of geography or politics but of time. Collectively, they tell a little-considered part of the history of a people perhaps uniquely tied to a particular piece of technology. Each on its own is a window into the lives—and deaths—of those who experienced that history firsthand. As such, it is my hope that each short vignette that follows might serve as a meditation on the risks we choose to live with, as well as on the losses that are part of the story of all that we have gained.

Unlike the question of guns in the present, their role in the past is apolitical. In previous centuries, guns were necessary—for sustenance, for home defense, for use within the Second Amendment's "well regulated militia"—in a way that some would argue they no longer are. Yet as tempting as it might be for gun-control advocates to seize upon the stories told here as evidence of how little our gun-obsessed culture has changed, it is not so simple. To begin with, as the frequently exploding firearms in many melancholy accident reports attest, guns themselves are infinitely safer objects than they used to be.

To the two-year-old digging through his mother's concealed-carry purse in Kootenai County, however, the relative safety of modern firearms is irrelevant, just as it is to the hundreds of other children across the country who have shot themselves or others since the #IdahoWalmart tragedy. The improvement of machines designed to kill has not broken the continuity between the past and the present—it has only reinforced it. While the gun as a symbol in American mythology has stood variously for revolutionary liberty, frontier-opening self-reliance, and most recently stand-your-ground security, hapless tragedy may be its most durable meaning.

In both the nation's early history and today, one thing remains certain: our relationship to these powerful, frightening, melancholy-making weapons is deeply personal. From childhood games of cops and robbers to the kinds of life-changing moments found on every page that follows, the marriage of guns and American lives endures.

Love them or hate them, they are a part of us. For better and for worse, we are all gun people now, just as we have always been.

THE TEXTS

Many of the accident reports gathered here were published and then republished in newspapers across the country weeks and even months after the incidents described. As a result, reports often included a variety of time frames and locations associated with a single event. In such cases, I have removed confusing multiple references to dates and places of publication. Otherwise, the reports appear here as they first did in print, complete with the finicky orthography and syntactical quirks of the day. The writers of the reports frequently used the abbreviations "inst." for "instant" and "ult." for "ultimo," to refer to the current month and the previous month respectively.

MELANCHOLY
ACCIDENTS

We have Advice from Lunenberg, that on the first Instant, a very melancholy Accident happened there. A number of Men in trying a new Gun by firing at a Mark against the side of a Barn, one of the Bullets struck upon some piece of Iron and split it (the Bullet) in two, one piece of which flew to a considerable Distance from the Barn, and upon a contrary line to its natural course, and struck one Dr. Rice (who was travelling the Road) in the Forehead or Temple, which wounded him to such a Degree, that he died about Nine o'Clock that Night. That piece of the Bullet that struck Dr. Rice was found in his Hat, the other piece (which flew quite a contrary way) fell down by the Rev. Mr. Stern's Door, where some Persons were standing but did no Hurt. However, Mr. Sterns sent the piece to the Men who were firing, with a desire that they would take more Care for the future.

New England Weekly Journal
BOSTON, MASSACHUSETTS

MAY 10, 1739

We have an account from Dursley, of a very melancholy Accident which happened there on Tuesday last, in the following Manner. Six young Lads of That town being out a shooting in the Fields adjacent, two of them shot at a Bird and killed it, and each claiming it as his particular Right, the Dispute grew so high, that they proceeded to Blows; and whilst three of the rest were endeavouring to part them, the fourth took up a loaded Piece, and said, Stand away, I'll warrant ye I'll part 'em, and immediately shot at them, whereby one was killed on the Spot, and the other so desperately wounded in one of his Arms, that 'tis dubious whether he'll ever recover the Use of it. The Coroner's Inquest have since sate on the Body of the deceased, and brought in their Verdict, Accidental Death.

The Boston Weekly News–Letter
BOSTON, MASSACHUSETTS

PHILADELPHIA. We have an Account of a melancholy Accident that happened on Thursday last in the Evening, in Burlington County, near Anchocas; viz: Two Neighbours going out to hunt Deer, unknown to each other, one of them, named James Sherron, passing through a bushy Place, the other observing something to move among the Bushes, and supposing it to be a Deer, fired at him, and the bullet entered his Breast and out his Back, but he run three or four Paces and fell down dead, the other perceiving to run made after it, where he found, to his great Surprize, the said Sherron dead. It is also remarkable that this said Sherron was shot at by the same Person twice before and badly wounded, but through Mercy escaped with his Life.

The American Weekly Mercury
PHILADELPHIA, PENNSYLVANIA

On Tuesday last, a very Melancholy Accident happened. A Gentleman, a Merchant was observ'd to be somewhat Melancholy, and at Times acted and express'd himself so as to cause those that were about him to suspect that he was not of sound Mind, and for that Reason, his Brother and a Gentleman intimately acquainted with the unhappy Man, agreed to be with him and perhaps more to divert him from the Melancholy thoughts which he entertain'd on Account of some disappointment, by their Conversation, than to prevent the Tragedy which ensued. The Night before the Fatality he seeme'd to be very uneasy and under several Pretences endeavor'd either to get out of Doors, or to get his Brother and Friend out of Doors, such as Fire, Thieves, &c. but failing in this he endeavor'd to separate them by using his Brother harshly, but was every Time quieted and put to Bed again. Very late in the Night, or rather early in the Morning he was heard to Grope for the Keyhole of his Chest, which was near his Bedside, upon this the Gentleman more to divert than any thing else, desired he would take care of the Sangery, he answered that he would and by the Ruffling of his Bed Cloath they thought him lain down again; but soon after a Pistol went off, and when they had lighted a Candle, to their no small Amazement they found him weltering in his Blood.----- The Explosion of the

Pistol was so vehement that it separated a Piece of his Scull, nearly of the Bigness of a middling Palm of a Man's Hand; this was found on one Side of him, and the Pistol on the other. The Coroner's Inquests have brought in their Verdict: Lunacy.

———•———

The American Weekly Mercury
PHILADELPHIA, PENNSYLVANIA

❦

NEW YORK. Monday Evening last, a very melancholy Accident happen'd in this City, when a young Gentleman having been on board the Clinton Privateer, then going out, had a Pair of Pistols given him; which on his coming on Shore he carried into a Publick House, among some of his Acquaintance, where one of them was found to be loaded; upon which several Attempts were made to discharge it; but missing Fire, he sat down in order to amend the Flint; in doing of which, the Pistol unhappily went off, and shot Mr. Thomas Cox, Butcher, through the Head, in such a Manner that some of his Brains came out, and fell down dead without speaking a Word.

The Pennsylvania Gazette
PHILADELPHIA, PENNSYLVANIA

WILLIAMSBURGH, VIRGINIA—Monday last being the Anniversary of his Majesty's Coronation, the following melancholy Accident happened in this City: At Noon when the Guns were fired, one of the Persons employed, loading one of them again too hastily, after it had been discharged, the Cartridge too Fired, and went off, by which his right Arm was shivered to Pieces, and obliged to be cut off, but we now hear he is in a hopeful Way of Recovering.

The Pennsylvania Gazette
PHILADELPHIA, PENNSYLVANIA

LONDON—Yesterday Morning a melancholy Accident happened at Mr. Pereira's, a Jew Merchant in Mark lane; Part of the Family being just come out of the Country, the Servants left their Pistols on a Table, which two Sons of Mr. Pereira being at Play with, one of the them shot his Brother through the Body, of which he instantly died.

The Maryland Gazette
ANNAPOLIS, MARYLAND

❦

From Pequea we have an Account of the following melancholy Accident happening there on Friday last, occasioned by a Person, who had been a gunning, and stopping at the House of one Mr. Cowan, left his Piece standing at the Door loaded, which was accidentally thrown down by a Child, and the Lock striking on the Threshold, it went off, and shot Mrs. Cowan under the short Ribs, of which she died, and has left disconsolate Husband, and five young Children.

The Boston Gazette, or Weekly Advertiser
BOSTON, MASSACHUSETTS

SEPTEMBER 26, 1754

❈

This Morning a melancholy Accident happen'd; a Dutch-man carelessly handling a Gun, it went off, and shot a Girl about 13 Years old thro' the Heart, and she instantly expired.

The Pennsylvania Gazette
PHILADELPHIA, PENNSYLVANIA

On Saturday last about two in the Afternoon, a Place call'd the Dust house, belonging to Mr. Norman's Gun-Powder mill, blew up; and kill'd one Man, who was barrelling up the Gun-powder. 'Tis reckoned there were about thirty Barrels of Powder in the Store-room, each Barrel containing about 100 lb. Weight. The building was blown into thousands of Pieces, and carried a great Way, the poor Man's Body was torn into so many Parts there is no finding them, or half his Bones. Seven or eight great Elms, that stood near this Room, were torn up by their Roots, and many others shatter'd, and several adjacent Buildings terribly torn: a Building about thirty Yards from it, which contained about the same Quantity of Gun-powder, had its Roof beat in, and a Man at Work received a slight Blow on the Back of his Neck, by a Piece of Timber, but the Powder remained safe. The Windows of several of the neighboring Houses were broke, and some of the Tiles blown off the Houses at some Distance, by the Force of the Shock. The Houses for many Miles about were shaken by the Explosion.

The Boston Weekly News-Letter
BOSTON, MASSACHUSETTS

LONDON: Saturday last a melancholy Accident happened to the Lord of Drumlandrig, eldest Son to the Duke of Queensbury, on his Journey from Scotland to Town: Being tired with riding in his Pose-Chaise, he quitted it and mounted his Horse, and riding over a plow'd Field in which was a great Number of Crows together, he drew out one of his Pistols from the Holster and cock'd it, with the Intent to fire amongst them; but at that instant his Horse made a Stumble, and his Lordship endeavoring to recover him, discharged the Pistol and shot himself dead on the Spot, to the inexpressible Grief of that noble Family. His Lordship had the Command of a Regiment in the Dutch Service, and was very lately married to a Daughter of the Earl of Hoptoun.

The Maryland Gazette
ANNAPOLIS, MARYLAND

❧❧❧

We hear from New Castle, about two Miles from this Town, of a melancholy Accident which happened there last Sabbath Day about 11 o'Clock before Noon, at the House of Deacon Jonathan Pierce's, in which one Josiah Furnald's Family lived; one Person being left at home to take care of the Children, who was obliged to step out to a Neighbour's House a few Minutes; and while she was gone, the Children got a Cannister of Powder about six pounds weight, which by Accident was left in that Room, carried it to the Fire, not knowing the consequence of Powder, put a Coal to the same, which blowing up, damaged the House very much, tore a Closet in the Room to pieces, and blew one of the Sashes out several Rods from the House, burnt one Child of four Years old in such a manner, that it died in a few Hours; and another Child of seven Years old it burnt in such a Manner, that its Life is not expected.

It is hoped this (and many of the like Instances which has happened by the Carelessness of leaving Guns loaded, and Powder in Children's Way) will be sufficient Warning to Persons to take Care for the future.

———•———

The New-Hampshire Gazette
Portsmouth, New Hampshire

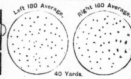

JULY 26, 1759

❧

ANNAPOLIS: Last Thursday Afternoon, a very melancholy Accident happened near Patuxent Bridge: A Number of Gentlemen having met there at an Entertainment, were firing of Guns, and in endeavoring to make three regular Reports with two Guns, that which was first fired was charged too soon with the Cartridge, and, in order to convey it quick down to the Breach, Mr. William Hamilton, Merchant, of Prince George's County (who had but just joined the Company) took hold of the Muzzle to shake it down, but as he was lifting it up, it went off, and mangled and tore away great Part of his Belly, so that his Entrails fell out, and he expired in a few Minutes. Another Man was thereby knocked down, but he recovered. Mr. Hamilton was a Gentleman justly esteemed, and his immature Death is much regretted, having left a young Widow near her Time.

———◆———

The Pennsylvania Gazette
PHILADELPHIA, PENNSYLVANIA

Last Thursday, a sad Accident happened at Wilmington. Five Children being left at Home alone in the House of Mr. Thomas Eavens, the eldest, a Girl of about 10 Years of Age, got down a Horn, in which was about a Pound of Gun-Powder, and to divert the rest, who were nigh the Fire, poured some of it out, which slushing into the Horn, immediately the whole took Fire, and burst the Horn. The Neighbors hearing the Report, ran in and found the Room dark with Smoke, and the Cloaths of the Children all in Flames; four of whom were burnt in a most shocking Manner; the Eldest so much, that her Life has been despaired of. But there is now some Hopes of her Recovery.

The Boston News-Letter
BOSTON, MASSACHUSETTS

On the 1st of this Month the following melancholy Accident happened at Norwalk in Connecticut, Mr. Daniel Seymour, Mr. Uriah Rogers, junr., and a Brother of his, a Boy, went out to shoot Pigeons. Mr. Seymour's Gun (unknown to him) had been cock'd, and thro' Forgetfulness was left so. In moving his Station, the Butt of his Gun was turn'd from him, and the Muzzle was brought against the upper Part of his Leg, at which Instant the Gun went off and broke the Bone to Pieces, tearing his Leg in a most terrible Manner, so that it only seem'd to hang by a few Ligaments; a considerable Number of shot (after passing thro' Mr. Seymour's Leg, as it was thot) struck the Boy in the Face, one of them just under his Eye. Mr. Rogers soon procured Help, and they were carried home. As the Boy also fell with the shot, and his Face was cover'd with Blood, it was thot he was mortally wounded, but upon Examination, his Wounds proved to be not dangerous. Mr. Seymour soon after the Accident said, he was sensible he should die; a Surgeon was procured as soon as possible and there was a Necessity to take off his Leg above the Knee, which was perform'd about Sun-set and an Hour or two after he expired, leaving a sorrowful Widow and several Children.

The Boston News-Letter
BOSTON, MASSACHUSETTS

LIVERPOOL. On Friday Afternoon, as Master Stephen Dubery, younger Son of Thomas Dubery, Esq.; of the Island of
Montserrat (a Youth of 10 Years of Age, sent over here for his
Education) was going to School along with his Brother, they
met a Boy about 9 Years old, belonging to the Ship Nelson,
with a Pistol in his Hand, and being acquainted with them
(not knowing that Pistol was loaded) he snapt it, and shot
Master Dubery with a Brace of Balls, which went through
his left Side, between Navel and Groin, and came out at his
right Buttock: He remained sensible some Time, declaring
the Innocence of his Acquaintance, the Sailor Boy, and died
on Saturday at 7 o'Clock in the Morning. This melancholy
Accident, we hope, will be a Caution against trusting loaded
Arms with Children. The Carpenter of the Ship was sending the Pistols by the Boy to be cleaned, without acquaint-
ing him that they were charged.

The Maryland Gazette
ANNAPOLIS, MARYLAND

❖

Last Wednesday a melancholy accident happened at Hampton in New Hampshire, as two men went out together to shoot at flock of Ducks, they agreed that as soon as the foremast fired, whose name was Green, the other was to take them rising, when Green's companion shot him thro' the head, and kill'd him immediately. He was a likely man, about 45 years of age, and has left a wife, and eleven children.

The Boston Evening Post
BOSTON, MASSACHUSETTS

A very melancholy Accident lately happen'd at North-Kingstown. A young Man at the House of Mr. James Sweet, going to clean a Gun that was loaded, of which he was unapprised, it unhappily discharged, and wounded a Girl about five Years old, Daughter of Mr. Sweet, who was in another Room, in so terrible a Manner, that after languishing two Days, she expired.

The Providence Gazette, and Country Journal
PROVIDENCE, RHODE ISLAND

SAVANNAH: On Friday last a melancholy accident happened at the plantation of William Port, a few miles from town. As one Mrs. Cox was going into one of the outhouses on the plantation, with some lighted sticks in her hand, unluckily some sparks of fire fell into a keg with about 20 lb. of gunpowder, which blew up part of the house, and burnt her in such a miserable manner that she died next morning.

The Georgia Gazette
SAVANNAH, GEORGIA

❖

NEWPORT—Last Sunday happened a most melancholy Accident at the House of Mr. Benjamin Dunham, at the Point Ferry-House, at about half after Two o'Clock in the Afternoon, viz. One of his Sons, a Child about Seven Years old, was sitting upon a Table, at which Instant another of his Sons, a Lad about Fourteen Years old, being in the next room, chanced to take up a Gun loaded with Goose Shot, to view it, when it immediately discharged, pierced through the partition, and shot the youngest in the Forehead, and some of the Shot came out at the back Part of his Head. He lingered till about Six o'clock, and died.

The Newport Mercury
NEWPORT, RHODE ISLAND

❧

AMWELL (NEW-JERSEY). On Wednesday, the 5th Instant, a melancholy Accident happened here. On the Afternoon of the said Day, Captain Daniel Reading, Son of
the Hon. John Reading, Esq., late of this Place, deceased,
and two other Gentlemen, each with his Fowling Piece,
charged with small Shot, went out to divert themselves, in
the Pursuit of Game in the neighboring Woods. And they
having discovered a Squirrel on a Tree, one of the Gentlemen presented; by the Object moving, he took down
his piece, and, as he confidently thinks, half-cocked it.
Whilst they were walking about the Tree in order to again
discover the Game, the Gun of the Gentleman who had
presented, being in his hand, accidentally went off, and
Captain Reading being at a little Distance in a Direction
nearly straight before the Muzzle of the Gun, and aptly
received the Charge in his Right Arm, rather above the
Joint of the Elbow, which not only lacerated the Flesh, and
fractured the Bone where it struck, but broke it off short,
a little above where it entered. With much Difficulty he
got home, in most excruciating Pain, which continued
for some Days. Skilful Surgeons were immediately called

to his Relief, who willing, agreeable to his own Desire, and that of his Friends, to use their utmost Endeavors to save his Arm, did not proceed to Amputation. Little or no Fever ensued, and after a few Days the Pain abated, and the wounded Part began to suppurate. But notwithstanding many flattering Symptoms of a favourable Issuence on the Morning of the 15th Inst., he unexpectedly and suddenly expired, without any visible Mortification in the Part, unless lined and blackish streaks under his wounded Arm, and on that Side, might be judged Indications of it.

Captain Reading's placid, easy open, benevolent, engaging Disposition and Conduct had rendered him the Object of universal Esteem and Affection where-ever he was known; hence his Death is very justly and greatly regretted! It is not only an unspeakable Loss to a deeply afflicted Widow, and a large Family of small Children, but to the particular Society to which he belonged, of which he was a very useful Member, and to all his Acquaintance. He was one of the most loving and affectionate Husbands, the tenderest of Fathers, a steady Friend; and his immature and unexpected Death in the Prime of his Days, and in the Midst of Usefulness, shews the Vanity of Man in his best Estate, and the great Necessity of attending to our Lord's Admonition, "Be ye also ready, for in such an Hour as ye think not, the Son of Man cometh."

It is said the Gun, which was instrumental in the above unhappy Affair, had sundry Times before gone off in the same unexpected and surprizing Manner.

————◆————

The Boston Post-Boy & Advertiser
BOSTON, MASSACHUSETTS

JULY 3, 1769

❖

We hear from Milton, That last Friday a Man at that Place in striking Fire with his Gun, not knowing it to be loaded, it went off just as his Daughter was entering the Door from Milking, and shot her through both her Thighs, of which Wounds she soon after died.

———

The Boston Post-Boy & Advertiser
BOSTON, MASSACHUSETTS

JUNE 4, 1770

BOSTON. Last Wednesday night a melancholy accident happened at Notamy, some young men, who had been a gunning, went to Beaman's Tavern, where one of their guns accidentally went off, and killed the landlord's daughter on the spot; she was at that time suckling her child, who was providentially preserved.

The Massachusetts Gazette
BOSTON, MASSACHUSETTS

JUNE 19, 1772

❧

We hear from Leicester that on Tuesday last a very melancholy Accident happened in that Town: A Son of Mr. William Henshaw, about 6 Years of Age, and another Lad being in a Chamber playing with a Gun, which they tho't not to be loaded. The Lad put the muzzle of the Gun to the Ear of Mr. Henshaw's Son, when it went off with a whole Charge of Partridge Shot, which tore his head to pieces, and killed him instantly.

The Connecticut Journal, and The New Haven Post Boy
NEW HAVEN, CONNECTICUT

◆

We hear from Taunton that on Wednesday the 4th inst. (it being their training day) the following melancholy accident happened there—Capt. Richard Cobb of that place, having loaded a gun very deeply, laid it on the ground, and discharged it with a fuse; the gun split, and a fragment of about eight inches in length struck him just below the knee and entirely separated his leg, leaving the remainder of the bones at the joint most miserably shattered. On the Saturday following, a consultation of surgeons being held, it was thought adviseable to amputate above the knee, he supported the operation with the fortitude of a hero, a character which he had justly merited by his intrepid conduct in the army. He survived the operation but a few hours, dying the next morning. He has left a disconsolate widow and children.

The Massachusetts Spy
BOSTON, MASSACHUSETTS

MAY 14, 1773

❖

NEW HAVEN—Last Monday the following melancholy Accident happened at the Parish of Farmingbury, in Waterbury. On the Morning of that Day (it being a general Muster of the Militia) a Number of young Men resorted to an Officer's House & as they enter'd the Door, they all discharged their Guns, but one Harrison, whose Piece would not go off—After they had been in the House a little while, Harrison took his Gun in Order to rectify the Flint, and not recollecting it was loaded, he snapt it, when it went off, and the Wad entered the Belly of one Abraham Byington, a young Man about 19 Years of Age, who was standing very near, by which he was so much wounded that he expired the same Day. Harrison and Byington were Fellow Prentices, near of an Age, and between whom there was great Intimacy and Friendship.

The Connecticut Journal, and The New Haven Post Boy
NEW HAVEN, CONNECTICUT

SEPTEMBER 19, 1774

A melancholy accident happened at Roxbury on Monday last, two young men diverting themselves with the military Exercise, when one of them gave the Word of Command to Fire! the other instantly discharged his piece, not knowing it was loaded, and the ball entered the head of his Companion, Mr. Henry Wilson, Baker, 22, and killed him on the spot.

SUPPLEMENT TO *The Boston Evening-Post*
BOSTON, MASSACHUSETTS

JUNE 24, 1777

NORWICH—A very melancholy accident happened at Go-shen last week, two young women, about fifteen years of age, being in a chamber together, where there was a gun loaded with buckshot, one of them taking it up, not knowing it to be charged, said she could take sight, and pointing the piece at the other, it being at half cock, went off, and killed her on the spot; there being a very great friendship between the two, the surviving one, very much affected at the sight, was deprived of her senses for some minutes.

The Pennsylvania Evening Post
PHILADELPHIA, PENNSYLVANIA

JUNE 29, 1779

WORCESTER—A melancholy accident happened last Friday at Sutton. Mr. Edward Severy and Mr. John Holman went out in a field in order to shoot birds; Mr. Holman presented his gun at a bird which flew away before he had time to fire, and in attempting to uncock his gun, it unfortunately went off and discharged the whole of its contents through the body of Mr. Severy, who was but about one rod distant. He died five hours after.

The Pennsylvania Evening Post
PHILADELPHIA, PENNSYLVANIA

✦

BOSTON: We hear from Weymouth, that last week the following melancholy accident happened there: As a number of young men were out a hunting, a musket accidentally went off, by the discharge of which one person was considerably wounded, and another, by the name of Lovell, instantly killed. Last Saturday afternoon, an unhappy dispute having arisen between one Curley and his wife, in Wings lane they came to blows, when he received an unlucky stroke from her, with the helve of an axe, and expir'd a few hours after. She is committed to gaol for trial.

The Norwich Packet, or The Chronicle of Freedom
NORWICH, CONNECTICUT

❖

Extract of a letter from Charlestown, South Carolina: A most melancholy accident happened in this city about an hour ago, Mr. Grattan, (a merchant here) was out from home: his two daughters and another young lady (Miss Guillideau) were in the store at work, when Miss Grattan's Brother, a boy about nine years old, came in, and seeing a gun, took it up and fired at the young ladies, which killed the youngest Miss Grattan on the spot and most dreadfully wounded his other sister, and Miss Guillideau. The unhappy boy immediately attempted to destroy himself, but was prevented: he was ignorant of the gun being loaded, and is now more composed. This, I think, is a sufficient warning to parents to not leave dangerous weapons in the way of children.

The Vermont Gazette, or Freemens Depository
BURLINGTON, VERMONT

MARCH 22, 1785

❖

LONDON: A very melancholy and most uncommon accident happened last week at a village near Highgate. Miss G., a young lady of fortune, being thwarted by her friends in her affections for a deserving man, shot herself with a pistol. The ball passed through her brain, and she died in an instant.

The Maryland Journal, and Baltimore Advertiser
BALTIMORE, MARYLAND

MAY 19, 1785

About a month ago, near Camden, a melancholy accident deprived a worthy woman of her life. Three men, who had been out a hunting, called at her house, where, as they were amusing themselves with their guns, and one of them continued to snap a loaded piece, to the apparent danger of his companions, she undertook, in a friendly manner, to expostulate with them on their rash impudence; upon which the foolish man threatened, with a jocular air, to shoot her, and presented his piece towards her, expecting it would only snap as it had done repeatedly; but to his great astonishment and distress, it went off, and discharged its contents into her neck, which killed her on the spot.

The State Gazette of South Carolina
CHARLESTON, SOUTH CAROLINA

The death of Thomas Foxcraft, Esq.; late Postmaster General in Philadelphia, was occasioned by a small coach gun, which he always travelled with, going off half cocked, whilst he was preparing to accompany some friends into the country. A man of more amiable manners or more benevolent disposition never existed.

Massachusetts Centinel
BOSTON, MASSACHUSETTS

RICHMOND: By a gentleman from Henry County, we are informed of a very melancholy accident which happened there some time since, William Hunter, in going out one morning to hunt, took a favourite son with him who was about 16; they had not proceeded far before they spied some turkeys on the side of a ridge; the father told his son to stay where he was and hide, till he went on the top of the ridge to intercept the turkeys if they proceeded that way, but the lad, not obeying his father, crept after him from some considerable distance, and got into the top of a tree which was full of leaves. The old man on his return, seeing something among the leaves of the tree which he took to be a turkey, fired, and observed something to fall (supposing it to be a turkey) went to pick it up, but to his great astonishment and grief found it to be his son.

The Maryland Journal, and Baltimore Advertiser
BALTIMORE, MARYLAND

AUGUST 31, 1786

❈

Friday last the following melancholy accident happened at Chelsea, as we hear, viz. A Son of Mr. Cheever, of that place, taking down a gun, not knowing it to be loaded, and snapping it at the door it went off, when the contents entered the body of one of Mr. Cheever's daughters, who languishes under misfortune.

Fowle's New Hampshire Gazette
PORTSMOUTH, NEW HAMPSHIRE

Extract of a letter from Bath: A melancholy accident happened about ten days ago, at a village near this city. A sheriff's officer had the temerity to open the window in the night, of the bedchamber in which a gentleman slept against whom he had a writ. Just as he entered the room, the gentleman awoke, took his pistol, and snapped it, but missed fire; he then seized a blunderbuss, which hung fire so long, that the officer had time to turn the muzzle towards the limbs of the unfortunate gentleman, and the whole contents were lodged in his thigh, so that he has lain ever since in a most deplorable condition.

The Charleston Evening Gazette
CHARLESTON, SOUTH CAROLINA

❖

The following melancholy accident happened during the military rejoicings on Thursday, the first day of the present session of the legislature. As Mr. Moses Pardee of this Town was ramming down a Wad into a loaded Cannon, the Charge took fire and he was instantaneously killed. He has left a wife and eight children to lament his awful death. -------When we who are living reflect, how often we have been in situations, apparently as dangerous as that of this unfortunate man, we may say with great truth, that it is by *accident* that we yet live; alarming consideration! ---- It should teach us to always be prepared for death, the time and circumstance of which are wholly beyond our knowledge.

The New-Haven Gazette, and the Connecticut Magazine
NEW HAVEN, CONNECTICUT

⬗⬗⬗

EXTRACT OF A LETTER FROM KNIGHTON, RADNORSHIRE

Mr. John Turner, junr., of Manaughty, in the parish of Bleathvaugh, near this town, set out Wednesday morning last, in company with another young man, to kill a few cocks; and on beating up by the side of the river they flushed a snipe. Mr. Turner's companion took aim, but his piece missed fire; and as he was backing the flint, Mr. Turner came up to him, rested his gun upon the ground, the muzzle reclining against his shoulder; in this posture he imprudently took out his flask, which contained a half a pound of powder, and attempted to prime his friend's gun, the whole flask blew up, and the explosion fired Mr. Turner's own gun, the contents of which carried away a part of his skull, and he dropped down dead. His companion was so terribly burned that he is dangerously ill. This accident, however unfortunate, was attended by a circumstance still more affecting.----
Mr. Turner's sister, a very amiable young woman, was that morning at Knighton, to which place the news was first brought. No sooner was she acquainted with her brother's fate, than she hastened home to her mother; but, on entering the house, overpowered with the misfortune, she fell on her knees, and bathing her mother's hands with her tears,

said, *O mother, this is more than I am able to bear!*, sunk down and instantly expired.

The distress of the family upon this melancholy occasion, is truly pitiable. The brother and sister are to be buried on Saturday in the same grave.

What a weight of affliction has one day brought on a very respectable family.

———◆———

Daily Advertiser
PHILADELPHIA, PENNSYLVANIA

POUGHKEEPSIE. On Wednesday evening last, a most shocking accident happened at the house of Mr. Jesse Oakly, merchant in the Nine-Partners. He having received five or six quarter casks of gun powder, with several other goods, and through hurry of business neglecting to secure the powder by conveying it from the store room, put it in a closet in one corner of it. Having several persons in the store with him, one of them taking a candle which had burnt in a manner to the snuff, unobserved by Mr. Oakly, let what was left of the candle fall into one keg, which taking fire instantly, blew up the whole—by which melancholy affair the person who had the candle, was torn to pieces, and one who stood next to him was thrown through the window into the street; another carried into the cellar, and there buried in rubbish, and the remainder in the store very considerable burnt and bruised—we are however, informed that they are all alive except the one who had the candle, though it is expected the person thrown into the street, and the one in the cellar will not recover—the rest are likely to do well, amongst who is Mr. Oakly. We sincerely regret that our merchants in general are too careless with this very dangerous article, and ardently wish this dreadful catastrophe may be duly regarded, and be a sufficient warning to those who keep the article of gun powder for sale. It appears to be very extraordinary that the powder when going off, carried away the corner of the store in which it stood, and instead of taking its course upwards, went through the lower floor in the cellar, where the most damage was done, by starting several hogheads liquors and half a dozen barrels of fish. The goods in the store were not much damaged, though the loss to Mr. Oakly is supposed to be near five hundred pounds.

———————

The New Haven Chronicle
NEW HAVEN, CONNECTICUT

NEW HAVEN—Last Sunday two children of Mr. Timothy Bradley of Brandford, being left at home while their parents were at meeting, the eldest, a boy about eight years of age, got down a loaded gun and as he was playing with it, it discharged and killed the other child who was then lying in a bed. The charge tore the forepart of the child's head in a shocking manner, and set the bedclothes on fire. Query, ought a gun to be kept charged except in danger of enemies?

Hampshire Gazette
NORTHAMPTON, MASSACHUSETTS

❧

Friday the 5th inst., the following melancholy accident happened in this town: As Arnold Inman and Elijah Felt were in
the woods at the south part of this town hunting wild turkeys,
it was in the twilight of the evening before they found their
game. One of them fired his piece and wounded one of the
turkeys; they both ran to catch it; Felt got hold of the turkey's
neck, when Inman was about ten yards distant advancing toward him, when Inman's gun went off (he says) by accident,
which was deeply loaded with large shot, some of which were
as large as pistol balls, the contents of which entered Felt's
legs; 14 shot entered his right knee, and but three or four of
them came through. The left leg was universally destroyed;
the shot entered just below the Patella; the Tibia and the Fib-
ula, in the space of 6 or 8 inches, were judged to be broken
into 50 pieces; and the Muscular parts entirely destroyed.
Yesterday a number of surgeons were called, who unani-
mously advised to an immediate amputation; which was performed by the ingenious Dr. Asa Hamilton of this town. The
surgeons hope that the other leg, with his life, may be saved.

The Boston Gazette, and the Country Journal
BOSTON, MASSACHUSETTS

❊

A melancholy accident happened on Monday last at White's Hotel, in Falmouth; a sea–faring lad, who had been in the house a few weeks, was in the kitchen with a servant girl, where a musket had lain for several months, and no person, from its being so foul and rusty, ever knew that it was loaded; the boy, in exercising the gun, placed it close to the girl's head, when it immediately went off; the contents of which were lodged in the poor creature's head; she instantly expired.

———

The Pennsylvania Packet, and Daily Advertiser
PHILADELPHIA, PENNSYLVANIA

❧

A gentleman from the northward informs that on the 29th of October last, the following melancholy accident happened in Georgia, in this State; It being a day appointed for training, early in the morning a number of young men went to the house of one of their officers, in order to give him a morning gun, the first man fired his piece, the second missed fire, which being likely to render their intended salute irregular, the third immediately discharged his piece, when the whole contents entered the side of the second man, which broke his third and fourth rib, and in a few hours put an end to his existence. The name of the deceased was Francis Ferguson; about 21 years of age. He has left a mother and sister in Albany, and a brother in Georgia, to lament his death.

> *Death wields his dart, and strikes the blow,*
> *Alike unfeeling for the high and low.*

The Country Journal
BENNINGTON, VERMONT

A melancholy accident happened a few days ago. A gentleman being seized in the night with a delirium, imagined he was beset by robbers and assassins, and making a great noise, a servant and his own son got out of bed and entered the room, upon which he discharged a fowling piece at them, and wounded his son, who lies without hopes of recovery.

The Pennsylvania Packet, and Daily Advertiser
PHILADELPHIA, PENNSYLVANIA

❖

NEW BRUNSWICK—A melancholy accident happened a few days since near Passaick Falls—Two brothers, together with a number of others, went a gunning in the morning: After having spent the day in social pleasure, and on their way home they were overtaken by a waggon, in which as many as could took seats, among the number was one of the brothers, the other remained on foot, when he offered to hand his gun to his brother in the waggon, which went off and shot the brother in the waggon through the body—he uttered but one groan and expired without speaking a word. It is said, the surviving brother could hardly support himself when called before the Coroner's inquest to be examined, on account of being the unhappy instrument of his own brother's death.

———◆———

New York Packet
NEW YORK, NEW YORK

Last Tuesday a lad by the name of Whittlesey, being on a visit to an intimate friend of his in Saybrook, named Lord, who informed him he had a new gun and desired him to examine it; on Whittlesey's taking the gun he enquired if it was loaded, and being answered that it was not, he snapped it in such a direction that a full charge of shot entered the breast and head of Lord, which instantly deprived him of life. On examination it appeared that the gun had been loaded in Lord's absence and that neither of the young men knew it previous to the melancholy accident.

The Hampshire Chronicle
SPRINGFIELD, MASSACHUSETTS

❖

LONDON—Last week two melancholy accidents happened from fowling pieces. A gentleman at Ellesmere, in Shropshire, accidentally shot his brother-in-law; and a young woman in Worcestershire was killed in the kitchen by a fellow servant, who was ignorant that the gun he was pointing at her was charged. These, with a hundred such like accidents, show the dreadful consequences of leaving loaded guns about a house, and of inattention and carelessness in the handling of them.

———◆———

Maryland Gazette
ANNAPOLIS, MARYLAND

❧

PORTLAND—A melancholy accident happened here the 4th inst.—Peletiah Wescott, Joseph Wescott, and Samuel Avery, came on shore from the schooner Freedom belonging to this port, to take off some things belonging to a gentleman going passenger in the vessel. A musket was among the articles, which was not primed, and which they supposed not charged—After the boat left the shore, Pel. Wescott took up the musket snapped it several times over the side of the boat, and then began to perform the manual exercise, and Avery gave him the word; when he came to the word, he snapped the gun, which proved to be charged, and the contents were lodged in the head of Avery, just above the right eyes—It blew off part of his skull and he expired in a few minutes. Wescott says that when he snapped the gun, it was elevated about Avery's head, but in bringing it to a priming position, it went off—this appeared the more probable, as the gun had been loaded some time before, and it is likely had become a little damp. No evidence appeared to the jury of any design in Wescott, on the contrary, every circumstance was favourable. The jury was unanimous in the verdict "Accidental Death."

The Daily Advertiser
NEW YORK, NEW YORK

❖

MELANCHOLY ACCIDENT

On Friday the first inst. A number of persons assembled at the house of Mr. Asoph Brown at Waterford, for the purpose of diverting themselves by shooting at marks, when the gun of Mr. Jonathan Whitney, loaded with a slug, was accidentally discharged and the contents, passing obliquely into the house, entered the body of Mr. Abraham Conant, just below the shoulder blade, and lodged in some part of the trunk. He continued in extreme pain till the next Friday, when he expired.

He has left a disconsolate widow to lament the untimely death of a tender companion.

The Eastern Herald
PORTLAND, MAINE

❖

MELANCHOLY ACCIDENT

On Tuesday last, Mr. Thomas Pickering and his brother Mr. Nicholas Pickering 3d, the former aged 22, and the latter 19, both sons of Lt. Nicholas Pickering of Newington, went off in the river, in a float a fowling, each of them were in the act of firing at a flock of birds, the youngest brother's gun went off, and the other's flashed in the pan; but on bringing his gun down from a poise, it discharged its contents through the head of Nicholas, which put an instant period to his existence.

These brothers had always lived in the greatest harmony together; and were the joy and comfort of affectionate parents, with whom we sympathize on this sad event.

———

Haverhill Observer
HAVERHILL, MASSACHUSETTS

BRIDGEPORT, (CON.)—The following melancholy accident happened in Stratford on Friday last. A son of Mr. David
Curtis, of that town, had been out shooting ducks, and returned with one which he had killed. His mother came into
the room to see the duck, while the lad went into another
room to put up his fowling piece. As he went through the
door with the loaded piece, the trigger caught the door post,
and its contents were discharged into the breast of the unfortunate mother, who expired immediately. It is remarkable that with this same piece, and almost in the same way,
a man was shot dead, about twenty-two years since.

The Spectator
NEW YORK, NEW YORK

MELANCHOLY ACCIDENT

On Thursday last week, Mr. Israel Pulcifer and Mr. Israel Foster, of Beverly, being with their guns for game, the former accidentally discharged a load of shot into the body of the latter, who was only three or four yards from the muzzle of the gun, of which he died in about two hours, in 21st year of his age. It is remarkable that Mr. Foster narrowly escaped death in a similar manner some years ago, when he had the lower part of his face blown off by the discharge of a musket loaded with powder only.

The Spectator
NEW YORK, NEW YORK

◈

ANOTHER MELANCHOLY ACCIDENT

On the 17th Mr. Alexander Lee, in company with some other gentleman, went a few miles below the city, for the purpose of fowling. In one of the fields near Point-House, Mr. Lee, in attempting to pass a ditch, rested his piece on the ground, and placed his hand on the muzzle in order to assist himself over. Unfortunately the gun was cocked, and something touching the trigger, it went off: the charge entered his hand, and his arm being in an angle position, the shot passed thro' his wrist, and again entered just below the shoulder, where the whole lodged. He was brought home to his house in Gaskill street, and medical aid immediately procured; but an amputation was deemed impracticable, or at least, that it would not be attended with any beneficial effects, and no hopes were entertained of his recovery by the gentlemen who attended him. A mortification soon took place, and after languishing seven days in the most excruciating torture, he expired on Sunday morning last. Mr. Lee was a sober industrious man, and possessed considerable property, the fruits of his assiduity.

———

Philadelphia Repository, and Weekly Register
PHILADELPHIA, PENNSYLVANIA

MELANCHOLY ACCIDENT

TRENTON, JUNE 22. On the 18th a melancholy accident took place in this vicinity. Mr. Jeremiah Mahony, being exceedingly fond of his gun, taking it into his hand said in a joke to his wife, come out and I will learn you to exercise; upon which she took another gun into her hand that had been, without their knowledge, loaded by her brother in order to shoot some crows, which she carelessly held in her hands, and when she attempted to snap it, unfortunately went off, the whole load entered his head just under his left eye, and went out just behind his right ear, and he fell lifeless at her feet. He was about 23 years of age, and she about 17; they had been married a fortnight the evening before. The distressing scene is not easily described, as an uncommon fondness had subsisted between them. An inquest was held over the body, and the jury returned their verdict, that his death was occasioned by the accidental discharge of a gun in the hands of his wife.

Maryland Herald
EASTON, MARYLAND

❧

SPORTSMEN TAKE CAUTION!

A melancholy accident happened a few days since at Kinderhook, when Mr. Beverly Bennett, a promising young man of the age of 23, was shot to death in the following manner. With some other young men he was setting off on a fowling party, some of whom were pushing off a canoe, in which a gun was laid, the lock supposed to be half cocked, when the motion of the canoe shaking the piece, it went off and discharged its contents into Mr. Bennett's head, blowing out his eyes and entering the skull, upon which he fell dead on the spot. On repairing to the scene of distress, his mother was so shocked at the spectacle that she fell into fits, which continued upon her five hours, when she was revived by medical assistance, and is yet living, though in great distress. Under the affliction of Mr. Bennett, the father of the deceased, his consolation is that:

> *Heaven sends misfortune; why should we repine?*
> *'Tis heaven has brought me to the state you see.*
> *And your condition may be soon like mine.*
> *The child of Sorrow and of misery.*

The Spectator
NEW YORK, NEW YORK

❄❄

The spider's most attenuated thread,
Is cord, is cable, to man's tender tie.

Melancholy Accident.—On Friday last, *Henry Selden*, aged 13 years, son of Mr. Joseph D. Selden, of this village, left home for the purpose of hunting pigeons. Not returning in the evening, his parents were much alarmed; but flattered themselves that he had fallen in company with a young man who was also absent, and that they had tarried the night, that they might be on the ground for hunting in the morning. The latter, however, returned at about noon on Saturday, without having seen the former. The people then collected and commenced a search for him.—They had not proceeded far, before he was discovered on the side of a ledge of rocks and half a mile east of the village, and lifeless. From the situation in which he was found, it is presumed that he had discovered some game at the top of the ledge, which is so steep as to be almost inaccessible, and was endeavoring to approach near enough to make a shot. To facilitate his ascent, he had left his shoes a little distance below. His gun was standing several feet above where he was lying, and in an erect position against the side of the ledge; which renders it probable that he first climbed up the rock, and while in the act of drawing his gun after him it went off. The contents entered the side of his head, and must have put an immediate period to his existence.

———◆———

Albany Gazette
ALBANY, NEW YORK

+∰+

MELANCHOLY ACCIDENT

On Monday, the 23rd of October last, Mr. Ira Sweet, be-ing in the house of Mr. George Tuttle, of Winchester, who was his neighbor and intimate friend, took a musket into his hand, which was in the room, and having sat down in a chair, laid the musket across his knees, he then opened the pan, as he says, and seeing no powder therein, impru-dently cocked and snapped the piece which discharged its contents (being loaded with common shot) through the neck and lower part of the head of a sprightly boy, three years and five months old, the son of Mr. Tuttle, and who sat within a few feet of the muzzle—An instant period was put to his life.

On recital of such shocking occurrences, it is the duty of all people to consider the consequences of the common heedless use of firearms. View the scene which took place in the above case, and similar to the too frequent cases of the like nature—There were several persons in the house; the mother in an adjoining room, hearing the tremendous roar of a gun in the midst of her family, succeeded by the shrieks of those present, exclaimed, "Somebody is killed, who is it?" She was answered in a frantic tone, "It is your son." She was met in a cloud of smoke by the agent, with the lifeless boy in his arms; his head hanging down with large streams of blood pouring therefrom. The parental agonies in such cases, will admit no description or consolation.

The Supporter
CHILLICOTHE, OHIO

Melancholy Accident—We are informed that Mr. Elias White, of Westhampton was accidentally shot on Thursday last by Mr. Jonathan Reeve, as they were hunting in the woods. They were in pursuit of a deer, and the unfortunate man was mistaken in the thicket for the animal. He has left a numerous and destitute family.

Suffolk Gazette
SAG HARBOR, NEW YORK

❦

Melancholy Accident—In the town of Scroon, N.Y. on the 14th a young man, named Adin Allard, about 17 years of age, son of Ebenezer Allard, was instantly killed by the discharge of a gun, in the hands of another young man, named Aaron Traver, son to Cornelius Traver. The circumstances were, that Allard was passing by the house of Traver, in the street, which caused a dog to bark. The night was dark. Young Traver went to the door, when he supposed he saw a dog or other large animal, about the door yard. He returned, took his gun, and again went forth, followed by a younger brother, with a light. Imagining he heard the animal in the road, he fired, and lodged 36 duckshot in Allard's face and neck, which instantly brought him to the ground, where he expired. These facts are gathered from what was related by the family of Mr. Traver. Young Traver has been committed to gaol.

———◆———

The Berkshire Reporter
PITTSFIELD, MASSACHUSETTS

❖

Melancholy Accident—At a hunting party in Pendleton Dis., S.C. on the 4th inst., captain Barkley William Findley, was unfortunately shot by the gun of his friend, which was accidentally discharged: his worthy family and numerous friends mourn his death.

———◄———

The Republican
SAVANNAH, GEORGIA

TRENTON: A most distressing accident befell Mr. Wm. Closson, of this city, on Monday last. He was with a hunting party a few miles from town; they had halted to take some refreshment, and Mr. C. was leaning with his left arm on his gun, when a dog, who was playing around him, unfortunately jumped with his paw on the trigger, and discharged the contents of the piece through the fleshy part of his arm, near the shoulder, completely separating the main artery. Mr. C. bled profusely until he fainted, when his companion succeeded in stopping the blood, and carried him to a neighboring house, where he was soon attended by Dr. Israel Clark, and in a few hours by Dr. J. T. Clark. After due examination and consultation, it was determined to amputate his arm, as the only probable means of saving his life; and the operation was accordingly performed. Mr. Closson is a worthy and industrious man, with a large family, and his misfortune is deeply regretted.

New Hampshire Intelligencer
HAVERHILL, NEW HAMPSHIRE

MELANCHOLY ACCIDENT

We learn from our correspondent in Bristol, that two young men landed on Popasquash, from a boat, in pursuit of game. After ending their excursion, they returned to the boat. One of them, Mr. Sylvester Munro, Jun., in reaching his musket to the boat, with the muzzle pointed toward him, it hit against the thwart, and discharged its contents into his abdomen. He survived but a few hours. He was a valuable young man, in the 17th year of his age.

Rhode-Island American
PROVIDENCE, RHODE ISLAND

⬥

Melancholy Accident—A Young woman of Providence, Rhode Island, was shot on the 12th of January last by the accidental discharge of a gun in the hands of Mr. Thomas Hammond, who was fixing the lock.

Concord Observer
CONCORD, NEW HAMPSHIRE

A *Melancholy Accident*—On the 31st day of January, a young man by the name of Charles Phillips, about 20 years of age, left his home, the house of his father, to go into the woods to cut wood, he took his gun with him, and told his parents that perhaps he might see some game. A short time after, his axe was found sticking in a tree in the woods near a wood road, about two miles from Columbia, in the township of Knowlton, and about half a mile from his father's house. He did not return that evening nor next day. On the morning of the 2d of February, he was found in the woods about one mile from his father's house, lying with his gun at his feet, the ball from which had pierced through his breast, and come out at the blade of his left shoulder. A jury of inquiry was immediately held over the dead body by James Vankirk, Esq., the jurors reported the death accidental and by misfortune. He was a young man who was remarked for his tenderness towards his aged and helpless parents, and was their whole dependence for their support. On the 3rd a funeral sermon was delivered by the Rev. Mr. Low, and a number of his friends and relations followed him to the grave.

Commercial Advertiser
NEW YORK, NEW YORK

❖

Sarah Johnston, daughter of Mr. Daniel Johnston, of Morris township in this county, aged about 17 years, was killed on Saturday evening the 24th by the accidental discharge of a rifle gun, loaded with a ball, while her brother was in the act of putting the gun away. We are unable to give a particular account of this melancholy accident—we learn that the gun was subject to going off at half cock—thus has a tender and affectionate father and mother been deprived of a fine girl in the bloom of youth.

A boy in Hopewell township was lately killed by the discharge of a loaded gun by another boy—as there is a trial pending we forbear making any remarks.

Washington Reporter
WASHINGTON, PENNSYLVANIA

✺

Melancholy Accident—A correspondent at Plymouth county acquaints us that on the late election day, a son of Mr. Oliver Leach of North Bridgewater was accidentally shot and expired in the course of twenty minutes. A lad in company with the deceased was attempting to uncock his gun, when it discharged, and the contents entered the unfortunate youth. "Such," adds our correspondent, "are the effects of allowing boys to handle fire arms, before they know how to use them."

The Essex Register
SALEM, MASSACHUSETTS

❦

Distressing Casualty—On Friday night, the 16th inst., John
Plott, jr., of Cabarrus county, in discharging his gun in the
dark to scare some vagrant wretch from the premises, accidentally shot his mother. The circumstances which led to
this melancholy catastrophe, we learn from a correspondent
are these: The premises of Mr. Plott, the father of the young
man, had been visited by some rogue, who at various times,
as was believed, had taken corn, and other things which
could be easily stolen. On the night abovementioned, about
12 o'clock, the dogs kept up an incessant barking, which
awoke the young man, who when he arose, took his gun, &
stepping outside the door, discharged it in the direction of
the noise; on entering the house, it was ascertained that his
mother was not in bed, and the family becoming alarmed,
a search was commenced for her. After searching the different houses, they proceeded in the direction which he had
fired, and their fears were soon too fatally realized. She was
found lying speechless, the ball having struck her on the
temple. Surgical aid was immediately procured; but little
hope was entertained that it would be of any avail. She had
probably gone out, at that time of night, to look after some
clothes that had been washed the previous day and were
hanging out to dry, and to secure them from the prowler;
and that wretch, whoever he may be, must be considered

the guilty cause of her untimely fate—should death, as is but too probable, be the result. Mrs. Plott is an amiable woman, a kind and affectionate parent, and highly respected and esteemed by all who know her; and this melancholy event has shrouded her family, who best know how to appreciate her worth, and to whom her loss will be irreparable, in the deepest affliction.

———•———

The Raleigh Register
RALEIGH, NORTH CAROLINA

✦

Melancholy Accident . . . As Nathaniel Ellicott Force was in the act of cocking and raising a gun, it unexpectedly discharged its load, the butt end giving him a violent blow in the bowels. The gun had been heavily loaded, with nearly double the usual proportion of shot, for the purpose of shooting on the wing. Medical assistance was immediately obtained, but proved to no avail. He lived about twenty-four hours after the accident occurred in extreme suffering.

New York American
NEW YORK, NEW YORK

NOVEMBER 13, 1838

MOST MELANCHOLY ACCIDENT—A very promising son of Capt. Moore, about 16 years of age, of the London Packet ship Westminster, was shot, a day or two since by the accidental discharge of a gun while on a visit from school to his home, in Lyme. He was shooting ducks, and in the act of raising his gun from the bottom of a boat, when the lock came in contact with the thwart, which caused the charge to explode, and the contents was lodged in his body. He survived but six hours. What renders the catastrophe peculiarly afflicting, his father and mother are now absent in England, and are yet to learn the heartrending tidings of the tragical fate of their child.

The Hudson River Chronicle
OSSINING, NEW YORK

❦

MELANCHOLY ACCIDENT—We learn from the *Hagerstown Torch Light*, that on Thursday last, Mr. Christian Winter, of that place, accidentally shot his eldest son, a promising boy about 8 years of age, through the head. The ball entered on the left side, a little in front of the ear, and passed out the back of the head, carrying a portion of the brain and skull along with it. The child continued to breathe for fifteen or twenty minutes, when it expired. Mr. W. was examining a pistol, which accidentally went off, the ball passing through the thin part of his own hand, through the child's head, slightly wounding a young man in his employment in the arm, and lodged in a portion of the room in which the accident occurred.

The Sun
BALTIMORE, MARYLAND

❖

FATAL ACCIDENT—C. S. Smith, Esq., editor of the Vidalia (La.) *Intelligencer*, while hunting on the 25th ult., accidentally shot himself. He died in a few hours. Upon hearing of the casualty to C. S. Smith, says the *Natchez Courier*, Mr. C. C. Forshey, his brother William, and two others, named Tibbles, started in a skiff, to proceed to the scene of his death. A violent storm came on, which prostrated a tree. In its fall the tree struck the boat, killing one of the Messrs. Tibbles instantly, wounding the other in the loin, and severely bruising William Forshey, one of the branches falling across his lap. Mr. C. C. Forshey escaped untouched. The other Mr. Tibbles is dangerously, but not, it is thought, mortally wounded, and William Forshey will no doubt soon recover without material injury.

———◆———

The Sun
BALTIMORE, MARYLAND

❖

Be cautious in handling your gun.—On the 2d inst. a young man belonging to Waterloo, Monroe co., Ill., named Constantine L. Omelveny, accidentally shot himself. He started from his father's on a gunning excursion, and previous to loading his piece, unconscious of its containing a load, placed his foot upon the lock to raise it, and put his mouth to the muzzle for the purpose of blowing in it to ascertain if it was clear; his foot slipped and discharged the whole contents into his mouth, killing him instantly.

The Times-Picayune
NEW ORLEANS, LOUISIANA

❖

SHOT BY ACCIDENT—A young man named Silas B. Howe, accidentally shot himself on board the North America, near Rochester, on Friday last, with a rifle he had loaded to kill squirrels. He was from Detroit, and in his pocket was a letter from his mother, with this caution—*"Silas, be very careful of your gun."*

———◆———

The Sun
BALTIMORE, MARYLAND

Shocking accident—On Sunday last, at Cottage Grove, about 8 miles from this place, a man by the name of Slaughter, accidentally shot himself with a rifle, while in pursuit of deer. We understand that three or four men were in a wagon together—they had discharged a double barreled gun at a deer, but without effect. Mr. Slaughter in a hurry caught hold of a rifle that lay before him, and while bringing it to him muzzle foremost, the lock came in contact with some things that caused it to go off, and shot him through the body. He died almost instantly. This is a serious warning to those who are in the habit of using these deadly weapons, to be careful.

Wisconsin Express
MADISON, WISCONSIN

Scientific American.

THE ADVOCATE OF INDUSTRY, AND JOURNAL OF SCIENTIFIC, MECHANICAL AND OTHER IMPROVEMENTS.

VOLUME 5.]   **NEW YORK MARCH 9, 1850.**   **[NUMBER 25.**

THE
Scientific American,
CIRCULATION 14,000.
PUBLISHED WEEKLY.
At 128 Fulton Street, New York, (Sun Building,) and
13 Court Street, Boston, Mass.

BY MUNN & COMPANY.
The Principal Office being at New York.
Barlow & Payne, Agents, 69 Chancery Lane, London,
Geo. Dexter & Bro., New York City
Stokes & Bro., Philadelphia.
E. Morris & Co., Southern.
Responsible Agents may also be found in all the
principal cities and towns in the United States.

TERMS—$2 a year; $1 in advance, and
the remainder in 6 months.

Rail Road News.

Indiana Railroads.

Some thirty-five miles of the Indianapolis and Bellfontaine Railroad, in Indiana, is nearly or quite ready for the iron. The Company have determined to lay the T rail, which they expect to provide early in the season. This portion of the track extends from Indianapolis to Andersontown, the County seat of Morrison County, and penetrates a fine agricultural region.

The Indianapolis and Peru Road has its superstructure completed from Indianapolis to Noblesville, a distance of twenty miles, and has recently made a contract at Pittsburg for iron to complete this portion of the road. The iron is deliverable in June, and the Company expect to be ready for the cars in October. The northern terminus of this road is Peru, on the Wabash and Erie Canal.

Both of these roads connect at Indianapolis with the Madison and Indianapolis Road, and will contribute largely to the business of this latter work.

The Knightstown and the Rushville Roads, both of which connect with the Shelbyville Road, and by that with the Madison and Indianapolis Road at Edinburgh, are rapidly approaching completion. Both have full purchases of iron, and are rapidly laying it down. They will be ready for the cars early in the Fall.

Coal in Locomotive Engines.

We look, says the Mining Register, in sorrow at the terrible devastation made in our timber by the Reading Railway Engines. We are not about to complain that reasonable effort has not been made by that Company to discover some mode of burning coal so as to prevent the metallic destruction they attribute to its use. But inasmuch as the value of our coal is regulated in part by the convenience of timber for propping the mines, and as the Collieries of Schuylkill County already complain of the advantages which other coal fields possess, it is of the greatest importance that we be not placed in a still worse position, by cutting off our supplies of prop-timber. Is the acknowledged saving which would be made by our Railway of coal could be substituted for wood fuel, we have assurance that every means will be taken to put a stop to the present fearful consumption of our timber. And in this hope, we suggest the attempt to apply the hot-air principle as well under the grates, as in jets of air on the top of the fire. It would be easy to try it at small expense, and our experience in burning coal in ordinary stoves enables us to entertain great hopes that such fuel than that which could be substituted for wood, may be saved and the destruction complained of entirely abviated.

The New-Bedford Mercury states that Captain Timothy Colby in that city has a bed-cord made of whales' sinews, which has been in the Colby family since 1646—509 years and has been used by Timothy Colby 41 years, and it is now as good as a dozen new hemp bed-cords. It has never been broken.

This Rifle is the invention of Mr. Christian Sharps, near of Mill Creek, Pa. It was patented in 1848. The simplicity of its construction, will be apparent by the following description.

Fig. 1 is a side view showing the cap box open. Fig. 2, is a section showing the interior of the cap box. Fig. 3 is a top or plan view. The same letters refer to like parts. The engravings represent the barrel and the butt broken off, (as every body understands such parts) in order to present enlarged and clearer views. A represents the wooden stock. T is the barrel ; B is the nipple or priming chamber communicating by a small collar with the charge in the barrel, N, in the hammer. The charge is put in at the breech, and the breech itself is a moveable steel back, J, that is pushed up like a wedge to back the charge in the barrel, and then drawn down to allow another charge to be inserted. There is therefore a strong metal chamber behind the butt of the barrel, and a broad slot in it, in which the moveable steel breech, T, is thrust

Fig. 2.

up and down. This sliding breech is secured on a swivel pivot, O, which moves the breech up and down for the purpose stated, by being operated by the handle, D, which moves on a center pin, C, thus allowing said handle to be drawn inwards to the butt (fig. 1) of the stock, when the breech is to be raised and pushed outwards (fig. 2) for the breech to be lowered for charging. To charge, the handle D is pushed forward, as represented in fig. 2, when the butt, S, is thrust along the groove, R, into the chamber of the barrel, when the handle, D, is drawn back, as in fig. 1, the sliding steel breech, J, is pushed up, wedging behind the charge, and it is then loaded ready for firing. It is designed for caps, and is self capping. This is done by the caps, E, being set on apics of a small moveable wheel, F, in the cap-box, P, as shewn in fig. 1. This wheel is taken out, armed around with caps, and set on to two small catches, M, which project out from each side of a barrel spring box, L. The spring is not shown, but it will be understood

to be attached to the box, L, inside, and in its screw arbor. The object of this barrel spring is to turn round the wheel, F, with the caps on it, towards the priming box, B. At K is a small iron plate, and behind it is a narrow channel, into which the caps are carried inwards, stripped off, one by one, as they pass through the channel behind the plate, H, and the one pushes the other forward above the small nipple opening, when the nipple, X, when rising, (as it forms part of the sliding breech) catches the cap, and thus caps itself. The wheel moves round one cap every shot, by one being exploded to make way for another to pass into the said channel. The wheel may be capped for 50 rounds. In fig. 3, is the inside of the spring barrel box, P, attached to the barrel box, L, there is a catch, B, shaped like an angular lever. This catch is for the purpose of holding the barrel box, under the plate, H, after it is wound up, to take off the wheel, cap it, and put it on again. It is then set free for the wheel to move gradually round. K is the lid of the cap box. This gun can be capped like another, without the self-capping

Fig. 3.

auxiliary action, and presents a breech-loading rifle of singularly simple construction.—This rifle can be loaded and fired nine times in one minute. Its accuracy is equal to the common rifle. The pistol, or patched ball can be used. It can carry half a mile with safety, and in one instance it was fired nine times in one minute and all the balls were placed within a circle of six inches diameter, at forty yards distance. Mr. Albert S. Nippes, is now making about 700 of them of the very best materials, and of superior workmanship. Orders addressed, (p.p.) to Mr. Nippes, Mill Creek, Manyunk Post Office, Philadelphia Co., Pa., will meet with prompt attention.

Useful Receipts.

Butter.

This is an article of domestic food, more of which is consumed in the United States than in any other country on the face of the globe. Good sweet butter, oh how delicious. It very often happens among families in our cities, that they will purchase good sweet butter at the stores, and which in a day or two becomes vitiated in taste. This is owing either to the manner in which it is salted and packed, or the manner in which it is kept after it is purchased. Much butter is spoiled from using salt containing lime and other substances which hasten its decomposition. Salt can easily be purified by pouring upon it a little warm water and allowing it to drain; it dissolves and takes out the lime and other extraneous substances, and leaves the salt nearly pure. The quantity usually added to butter is one ounce to the pound. After butter has become rancid, it can be restored and made nearly sweet by a very simple process. This is, to wash it well in cold water, often changed, and after pressing out the water, salt it anew and add a little sugar, say half an ounce to the pound. This will be found to render it much more palatable, although it may not entirely restore that delicate flavor peculiar to new and sweet butter, which once lost can never be restored.

Butter should be kept in a cool, airy, dry place. The majority of city pantries and cupboards appear to be designed for the purpose of giving the butter kept in them, that peculiar odorous flavor (so agreeable to a Hottentot) termed rancidity.

Simple Cure for Croup.

We find in the Journal of Health the following simple remedy for this dangerous disease. Those who have passed nights of great agony at the bedside of loved children, will treasure it up as an invaluable piece of information.—If a child is taken with croup, instantly apply cold water, ice water if possible, suddenly and freely to the neck and chest, with a sponge.—The breathing will almost instantly be relieved. So soon as possible, let the sufferer drink as much as it can; then wipe it dry, cover it up warm, and soon a quiet slumber will relieve the parent's anxiety, and lead the heart in thankfulness to the Power which has given to the pure gushing fountain such medical qualities.

Extreme Cold.

The Vermont Chronicle, published at Windsor, Vt., says, that, on the morning of the 6th ult., the thermometer fell in that village as low as thirty-five degrees below zero ; in Woodstock, thirty-eight, and at Northfield, forty.—In New York City, at 7 A. M., it was 16° above zero.

Colder Yet.

The Quebec Gazette says, that on the 5th ult., the mercury fell, at Fortneuf, on the St. Lawrence, 29 miles S. W. of Quebec, to fifty-two degrees below zero, and continued below forty during the whole day. In this city, it did not fall lower than 12 degrees above zero.

Warning for Apothecaries.

A young lady in Trenton, N. J., a few evenings since, (says the State Gazette,) experienced a narrow escape from death, by having administered to her a spoonful of cosmetic, which was sent from an apothecary's shop in a vial very improperly labelled assafoetida. The mistake was not discovered until the fatal poison was mostly swallowed, and the most agonizing pains ensued.

❦

Melancholy Accident—John A Hellings, late landlord of the steamboat hotel, in South Trenton, accidentally shot himself on Saturday last, on his farm, near Bristol, Pa. Mr. Hellings took his gun to the cornfield for the purpose, as he had informed his family, of shooting a crow. He had been gone but a few minutes when the report of his gun was heard, but of course no alarm was created thereby. Several hours having passed without his return, search was made, when Mr. Hellings was found lying beside the cornfield fence, shot entirely through the heart. The unfortunate man had climbed the fence, and in carelessly pulling the gun over afterwards, was shot as above described.

———◆———

Public Ledger
PHILADELPHIA, PENNSYLVANIA

ACCIDENTAL SHOOTING—Another unfortunate instance of the folly of trifling with fire-arms, occurred on Belle Isle, near Richmond, Va., on the 9th inst. A white man named Reese Cook, who resides on the island, had been out practicing with one of the Allen's patent six-barrel revolvers. On returning he jocosely remarked that he would frighten a colored man named Jerry, who was standing near. Supposing each barrel of the pistol to be empty, he raised it up in a line with the body of the colored man and pulled the trigger, the barrels commenced revolving, when one of them, unfortunately remaining undischarged, exploded, and the poor man was launched into eternity without a moment's notice. The pistol ball took effect in his back, and he expired almost instantly. A jury of inquest was promptly summoned over the remains of the unfortunate man, who rendered a verdict of manslaughter against Cook for carelessly trifling with the pistol. Cook was taken into custody, but permitted to give bail in the sum of $200 to answer the charge. The colored man, we learn, was a slave and belonged to the Belle Isle Manufacturing Company.

The Daily Picayune
NEW ORLEANS, LOUISIANA

❈

The body of a German was found near Buffalo in an advanced state of decomposition, which from the position of the body and a gun, is supposed to have accidentally shot himself while hunting. Name not known.

The Sandusky Register
SANDUSKY, OHIO

NOVEMBER 22, 1849

⁂

Accidental Shooting—At Demopolis, Ala., a few days ago, several little boys, under 9 years of age, got possession of a gun which was supposed not to be loaded, and, providing themselves with a box of caps, amused themselves with snapping the gun. After exploding nearly forty caps, one of the boys pointed the gun at another, told him he believed he would shoot him, and pulled the trigger, when the gun unexpectedly went off and killed the little fellow on the spot.

The Sun
BALTIMORE, MARYLAND

❦

Accidental Shooting—A German named Franz Deiderich, yesterday afternoon entered a gunsmith-shop, near the corner of Second and Spruce streets, to examine some guns, with a view of purchasing. He took up a double-barreled gun, tried one barrel with a view to ascertain whether or not it was loaded, and finding no load in the barrel, he placed a cap on the tube for the purpose of testing the power of the spring. By mistake, the cap was put upon the barrel which had not been tried. The gun was pointed out of the door, and the trigger pulled, when to the surprise of all a load was discharged. Mrs. Adeline Keachii, who chanced to be passing at the time, on the opposite side of the street, received the greater part of the charge in her breast and shoulder, and is not expected to survive. Deiderich was arrested, and the witnesses in the case sent before the grand jury.

Daily Missouri Republican
St. Louis, Missouri

DEATH OF A CITIZEN OF BROOKLYN IN CALIFORNIA

A correspondent of the *New York Journal of Commerce*, writing from San Francisco under date of May last, relates the following: —"A melancholy event occurred here last week. A young man from Brooklyn, L.I., having returned unsuccessful from the mines, was induced to take employment as a monte dealer, at $10 per day. While engaged one evening at his table, an altercation took place between his employer and one of the betters. The young man finding his employer getting the worst of it, handed him a loaded pistol, with which to defend himself. Hardly had the pistol left his hand, before it accidentally exploded, and the ball lodged in his abdomen. He died in three minutes, and the coroner rendered a verdict of 'Accidentally Shot.' His employer had him respectably interred."

Brooklyn Daily Eagle
BROOKLYN, NEW YORK

❖

Accidental Shooting—On Wednesday evening last Miss Eliza Hebbs, of Washington city, the eldest daughter of Charles Hebbs, of the pension office, was accidentally wounded in the left breast by a bullet from a pistol in the hands of Wilson Brown, an estimable young man, who was at the time on a visit to the house of Mr. Hebbs. They were standing together in the front door, when she playfully pushed the door against him, when the pistol was accidentally discharged, the bullet passing through the door and entering her breast. Had it not thus spent its force it must have proved fatal. The bullet has since been extracted and the lady is doing well.

Daily Ohio Statesman
COLUMBUS, OHIO

JULY 2, 1851

❖

Most Melancholy Accident.—A Mrs. Moreland was recently shot and fatally wounded, at Pelham, N.H., while struggling with her own son, a lad age sixteen, who had taken his fowling piece to go a gunning. She had forbid his starting until he drew her a pail of water, which he had refused to do.

The Times-Picayune
NEW ORLEANS, LOUISIANA

✦

Accidental Shooting. Mr. Josiah J. Marr, a machinist, of Lowell, while on a visit to North Monmouth, N.H., on Thursday, was accidentally shot dead. He, with others, was in a boat, and a night-hawk coming into view, it was proposed to shoot at the bird. A double-barreled gun was handed to one of the party, and as he was receiving it, the lock rubbed against the side of the boat, which caused its premature discharge, and the whole charge was lodged in the forehead of Mr. Marr.

Salem Observer
SALEM, MASSACHUSETTS

❄

MELANCHOLY ACCIDENT BY THE CARELESS USE OF FIREARMS.—We learn from a gentleman who came passenger over the Long Island Railroad, on Friday, that on Wednesday last, at Hoppogue, Smithtown, Suffolk County, a girl named LAVINIA CONLEY, 9 years of age, was mortally wounded, by the accidental discharge of a pistol, by a colored man, whose name could not be ascertained. The contents took effect in the forehead of the girl. The negro was arrested immediately, and held for examination.

The New York Times
NEW YORK, NEW YORK

❖

ACCIDENT—Mr. David Allen, of Mill Neck, Oyster Bay, who had missed a quantity of corn, set a gun in his crib to shoot the thief, when upon going in himself the next morning, Friday last, having forgotten all about it, he was caught in his own trap, the gun going off and lodging a charge of shot in one of his knees. It is probable that it will have to be amputated.

Brooklyn Daily Eagle
BROOKLYN, NEW YORK

DREADFUL ACCIDENT FROM THE CARELESS USE OF FIREARMS—Shortly after 3 o'clock on Saturday afternoon, a man named Patrick Murray, residing at No. 17 Washington St., accidentally shot his daughter, a child of 4 years of age, in the forehead with a pistol loaded with powder and shot, causing a wound which will probably prove fatal. It appears he took down the pistol, supposing it to be unloaded, and drew the trigger; the charge exploded and took effect in the forehead of the child. It was afterwards ascertained that a son of Mr. Murray had, unknown to the father, used the pistol and left it loaded. Immediately after the occurrence of the melancholy accident, two physicians were called to attend the child, whom they pronounced beyond recovery. She was then conveyed to the New York Hospital. The father was arrested by police captain Halpin of the 1st ward, and detained until the matter should be investigated, which was done on the same afternoon by Coroner O'Donnell, after which he was discharged from custody.

Brooklyn Daily Eagle
BROOKLYN, NEW YORK

APRIL 7, 1854

⬦

DISTRESSING AFFAIR—A young man named Hilles accidentally shot his sister last week, near Georgetown Cross Roads, Maryland, whilst trifling with his gun. He had the weapon in his hands, and pointed it at her, when she ran and he pursued her, and just as she went to close the door of the house, the gun accidentally went off, and the load entered her side. Her physician thinks she cannot recover.

The Sun
BALTIMORE, MARYLAND

❖

ENCAMPMENT OF THE NATIONAL GUARDS— MELANCHOLY ACCIDENT

The Seventh Regiment returned to the City on Saturday afternoon from their week's encampment at Kingston, and was received at the landing by the 71st Regiment, under the command of Col. Vosbourg, and looked finely, though of course somewhat jaded.

The encampment has been a very satisfactory and pleasing one throughout, with the exception of a melancholy accident which occurred there on Friday. The Regiment was going through the battalion movements, and all the different firings. The various companies had fired twice successively, and the whole left wing once, when the order was given for the right wing to load and fire. The order was obeyed with promptness, but scarce had the smoke cleared from the ground ere a piercing and heart-rending cry fell upon the ears of every one present, and it was soon found that a young country woman with her child had been shot by a call from one of the muskets. The unfortunate young woman was borne in the arms of several soldiers to the hospital tent, where upon examination, it was found that the ball had entered the right side of the left breast, about an inch and a half below the nipple, passing entirely through the breast, entering the left arm near the shoulder, frightfully fracturing the bones of the arm and again passing out. The child, an infant only six months of age, was picked up when the mother fell, covered with blood, which flowed profusely from a wound in its head. Upon examination by the surgeons, it appeared that the skull was fractured and a piece of the bone above the forehead carried away; the wound was about three inches long, and through the aperture the brain protruded. The brain was pressed back to its place and the wound closed, when the little sufferer was given to a nurse for better care.

As soon as practicable, the mother and child were removed to a hotel in the village, where the Regiment made every provision for the sufferers, and raised by contribution about $1,000 for their assistance.

The wounded woman is the wife of Jeremiah Cassell, who lives about six miles back of Kingston. The ball that injured her passed through the skirts of a young man's coat standing near, and in its descent tore the dress of a lady who was standing behind Mrs. Cassell.

Mr. Cassell, the husband of the wounded woman, was present at the time of the accident.

The officers state that all the muskets were carefully

examined before the firing, and inasmuch as each of the muskets had been already discharged three times, the accident, it is said, must have resulted from the negligence of some State official in the Commissary Department, placing a ball cartridge among the ammunition of the Regiment.

On the other hand it is thought the accident may have resulted from negligence on the part of some one of the soldiers, as several of the companies had been firing at a target with ball cartridge during the day.

The accident cast a melancholy gloom throughout the encampment, and in consequence of it the grand ball with which it was to have closed did not come off, but the Regiment received their visitors in the camp.

Strange as it may seem, the mother and child are both doing well, and neither of them will die of their wounds.

——————

The New York Times
New York, New York

⊶⊷

Melancholy Accident—On Monday, Mr. Wm. Graves, of Graves' Station, Chesterfield, Va., met with a melancholy accident while out hunting with his son. It appears from a statement on the Petersburg Express that they were walking along—the son before and the father following—when, by some accident, the gun which young Graves had upon his shoulder fell down a little behind, and his father, in catching it by the muzzle to prevent its falling to the ground, casually brought it to a level with his throat, when it went off, the whole content lodging in that part of his neck. He was killed almost instantly.

The Charleston Mercury
CHARLESTON, SOUTH CAROLINA

❈

MELANCHOLY ACCIDENT— LOSS OF LIFE

Yesterday afternoon, about 3 o'clock, a melancholy accident occurred at the house of Mr. Ballentine, on the Mission road. Messrs. John Cramer, Wm. P. Mullins and several others were spending the afternoon with Mr. Ballentine. Mr. Cramer, at the time above specified, found a double-barreled shot gun in a room adjoining that in which the rest of the company were sitting, and taking it, with his hand near the muzzle, dragged it, with the butt upon the floor, toward the company. It unexpectedly went off, the contents passing through the left leg of Mr. Cramer and into the face of Mr. Mullins, who was sitting opposite. The gun was loaded, as is said, with No 5 shot, which all passed through Mr. Cramer's leg below the knee, making rather a clean hole where they entered, but tearing and lacerating to a horrible extent where they passed out. The small bone of the leg was completely shattered, and the main arteries were injured. Mr. Mullins was seriously injured in different parts of the face, and one of his eyes is said to have been entirely destroyed. Medical assistance was immediately sent for, and several physicians from the city proceeded to the spot. Chloroform was administered to Mr. Cramer, whose wound was bleeding profusely, the injured arteries were taken up and a number of shattered pieces of bone extracted. All efforts to preserve his life, however, were unavailing, and he died last night about ten o'clock. Mr. Mullins will doubtless recover, but not without being badly disfigured in the face. The accident seems to have resulted entirely from carelessness, whatever may have been the immediate cause of the discharge of the gun, which is said by some to have occurred in a stumble by Mr. Cramer, and by others to have resulted from the gun hammer catching on the door sill between the rooms.

Daily Evening Bulletin
SAN FRANCISCO, CALIFORNIA

SEPTEMBER 10, 1857

※

Last fall the State of Iowa dispatched Professors Moore and Francis to Ecuador to make certain scientific explorations. These gentlemen have been in that country since November last prosecuting their researches. They had left Quito, and were making their way toward the Amazon, intending to return to the United States by that route. They had stopped for a few days at an Indian settlement on the banks of the Napo river. During their stay there, Professor Moore accidentally shot his friend and companion.

Whilst in the act of cleaning his gun, it went off, and its contents of buckshot entered the breast and neck of Professor Francis, which caused his death in a few days. As may be expected Professor Moore is greatly distressed. He at once asked for an investigation of the matter, which has been had, resulting in acquitting him of blame. Our resident Minister at Quito is in possession of all the facts connected with this melancholy affair, as well as the judicial proceedings had in the premises, and doubtless will forward them to our Government at Washington.

———————

Richmond Dispatch
RICHMOND, VIRGINIA

❦

Melancholy Accident—Two young men, residing in this parish, were playing with gun, on the north side of the Red River, on Wednesday last, when one of them, named Ketz, accidentally shot his companion, Jenkins, who fell mortally wounded and expired in about an hour afterwards. We have heard no particulars of the melancholy occurrence.

The Times-Picayune
NEW ORLEANS, LOUISIANA

❖

A Mother Accidentally Shot—A young man named William C. Carroll, residing at No. 276 Hudson Street, New York, accidentally shot his mother on Friday, wounding her so severely that it is thought she cannot recover. He was preparing a pistol to shoot some rats, and while putting on a percussive cap, the pistol was accidentally discharged. The ball entered his mother's back, near the right shoulder blade, and passed through the right breast. She is sixty-one years of age.

———

The Poughkeepsie Eagle
POUGHKEEPSIE, NEW YORK

AUGUST 11, 1859

❦

FATAL ACCIDENT—Mr. John S. Sumner, who lives about four miles northeast of Pine Grove Village, Mercer county, accidentally shot his wife last Saturday morning, under the following distressing circumstances. Mr. S. had taken down his gun for the purpose of shooting some birds that were destroying his peas in the garden. As he approached the birds, they flew away. He returned to the house and proceeded to hang up his gun, and while doing so, the hammer of the lock caught in a crack in the chamber floor, and as it slipped off, discharged the weapon, the contents entering his wife's head and killing her instantly.

———◆———

Pittsburgh Daily Post
PITTSBURGH, PENNSYLVANIA

JANUARY 14, 1860

❖

On the—ult., Thomas Wilson accidentally shot himself, and bled to death ere medical assistance could be procured from Fort Yale. It appears that his object in coming down was for the avowed purpose of writing and sending $100 to his mother in Philadelphia, of which city he was formerly a resident. The melancholy accident occurred whilst he was crawling under a fallen tree, keeping the gun upon his shoulder, stock up and barrels pointing down, when the hammer came in contact with the log, discharging the contents into the right leg above the knee.

————◆————

Daily Alta California
SAN FRANCISCO, CALIFORNIA

JUNE 14, 1860

❧

A Little Girl Shot—We have just been informed that a little boy, son of a Mr. Evans of Cass county, residing some ten miles south of this place, accidentally shot his little sister. The following are the facts as we have learned them. The little boy aimed to shoot a bird, not noticing his little sister, who was in the range of the gun. The ball entered the back and passed out at the breast, dangerously wounding her. No hopes of her recovery.

The Plymouth Weekly Democrat
PLYMOUTH, INDIANA

❖❖❖

I have just been witness to a very sad occurrence on Co. D. 7th Reg. A young man accidentally shot his intimate friend while they were lying together in their tent. He was loading his revolver, and dropped it, when it discharged, the bullet passing through the right lung of his companion who lie by his side. He will live but a short time. Privates should never be allowed to carry revolvers. They are the means of killing 20 of our men where they kill one of the rebels. Officers have no other means of defending themselves. A sword amounts to nothing in the hands of an inexperienced officer. But privates have guns and bayonets. A gun is worth a dozen pistols.

Western Reserve Chronicle
WARREN, OHIO

◆▦◆

TERRIBLE TRAGEDY IN BUFFALO

On Thursday morning, Moses Menard, a Frenchman, accidentally shot his wife under the suspicion that she was a burglar who had entered the room. He states that on his return home from the night before, he was informed by his wife that some men had endeavored to gain admission to the house during his absence. She persuaded him to load his gun, which he placed by the bedside. In his statement he says:

"I was woke by some noise in the morning, and found that the light on the table had been put out. It was almost dark in the room, but I could see somebody standing between the little table and the head of the bed. I was so excited that I didn't think of its being my wife—remembering what I had told her when I went to sleep—and snatched my gun from the corner, raised quickly, and with my back to the foot of the bed, fired at the shape. I didn't know whether I aimed at the head, or where. I heard a fall after I had fired, and getting up and slightly opening the front door to let the light in, saw it was my wife. The curtain over the window made the room so dark before."

The discharge of the gun attracted the attention of some officers who entered the house. The room was a small one, about fifteen feet square. At the further left hand corner stood a bed, and in front of the bed, prostrate on the floor, with face downward, lay the corpse of a woman. Half the upper part of her head was shot off, and a pailful of blood and brains surrounded it. The wall beside the bed, about six feet above the floor, was spotted with brains and perforated with shot, and a chair directly beneath held the mass of brains that had fallen. Standing just in front stood Menard himself, half dressed, and holding his trousers in his hand. In the middle of the bed lay an infant slumbering. Menard was taken into custody.

The Pittsburgh Gazette
PITTSBURGH, PENNSYLVANIA

❖

PAINFUL AND MELANCHOLY ACCIDENT

Yesterday, a most singular accident happened to the little son of Mr. Wm. H. Perry, a boy of about 3 years. He had gone into the yard for a drink, and a moment afterwards his mother heard him cry; when she went to him he complained of his leg, and on examination a wound was found, between the knee and the ankle, sufficiently large for a person's finger to be laid therein, and laying bare the bone. The wound must have been made by a ball from a gun in the hands of some reckless person shooting on or about the hills in that vicinity.

———◆———

Marysville Daily Appeal
MARYSVILLE, CALIFORNIA

❖

The Dangers of a Battle Field—There are many dangers connected with a battle field, even after "the hurly-burly's done, and the battle's lost and won." Loaded guns and small arms of all kinds, and unexploded shells, which burst with the slightest blow upon their percussion caps, lay thickly over the deserted field, ready to hurl death along careless saunterers and curiosity seekers. Several fatal accidents of this nature have already occurred at the scene of the late fight at Gettysburg. On Friday morning last, Mr. Solomon Warner, of York, who was engaged in hauling muskets off the field, was killed by the accidental discharge of one of the guns whilst unloading it. The ball went through the heart, killing him instantly. Edward M. Woods, son of Alexander Woods, living near Gettysburg, accidentally shot his brother one day last week, whilst playing with a gun picked off the battle field.

Reading Times
READING, PENNSYLVANIA

MELANCHOLY ACCIDENT.

A WIFE SHOT WITH A PISTOL IN THE HANDS OF HER HUSBAND.

A sad accident occurred on Sunday last, at No. 167 Third-street, whereby Mrs. Augusta Schmidt, wife of John Schmidt, lost her life. The following are the circumstances as testified to yesterday upon the inquest held by Coroner Naumann on the body of Mrs. S.: About a week since Schmidt loaned his revolver to a friend, and on Sunday last he went for it and took it home with him in the evening. Mr. Hark, the friend, had been threatened on Saturday night by some rowdies, and loaded the revolver, but having no occasion to use it, he left it in that condition. The latter was not at home when Schmidt called for it on Sunday, and a servant handed it to him. The husband took the pistol out of his pocket in his wife's room, and was about to hang it up, when it was by some means discharged. One ball entered the back of his wife, passed entirely through her body, and lodged in the groin just under the skin. From the effects of this wound she died soon after. Just previous to her death she made an affidavit before Coroner Naumann, in which she stated the circumstances substantially as above set forth. Mr. Schmidt has been ill for the last two years, and this calamity has affected him very deeply, rendering him almost beside himself. The mother has left four children, the eldest only seven years of age.

———◆———

The New York Times
New York, New York

❧❧

BROOKLYN CITY NEWS

A Soldier Accidentally Killed—John Conners, a soldier, who served in Major General Thomas' army, met with an accident on Sunday night, which terminated fatally. He had just come to his mother's house, No. 75 East Baltic street, from Chattanooga, and being anxious to prepare his pistol for the Fourth of July, attempted to draw out the charge, and in so doing it went off, and the ball passed through his brain. He was taken to the Long Island College Hospital, where he survived some hours, when death relieved him of his sufferings. Mr. Conners had participated in many battles, and escaped through all. An inquest was held by Coroner Lynch, and a verdict in accordance with the facts was rendered.

———◆———

The New York Herald
NEW YORK, NEW YORK

MARCH 6, 1867

A fellow at Milford, Kosciusko county, named Wiley, on last Tuesday, accidentally shot his brother, inflicting a serious wound. He was engaged in the Nasbylike pastime of shooting a negro, and missed his mark.

Indiana Herald
HUNTINGTON, INDIANA

A DISTRESSING ACCIDENT

A FARMER SHOOTS
HIS WIFE MISTAKING HER
FOR A BURGLAR

On Saturday night last, a farmer named James Moore, residing on the Weston road, about six miles below this city,
accidentally shot his wife, inflicting a very severe wound.

Mr. Moore is a very well to do farmer and at times has
had considerable money at his house. This fact was generally known, and on several occasions attempts were made
by burglars to enter the premises. The attempts were all
frustrated and Mr. Moore was generally on his guard and
prepared to receive unseasonable visitors.

On Saturday night, about eleven o'clock, while a heavy
snow storm was raging, Mr. Moore heard somebody at
the front door. He left his bed, armed with a revolver, and
started for the main hall. As he reached it, he heard the in-
truders leaving the premises, and at once started back to his
bedroom. In the meantime, his wife had left the bed and
was standing at the window looking out for the thieves. Her
husband, as a matter of course, supposed that she was still
in bed, and seeing a human form at the window, concluded

at once that it was a burglar about to enter the window, and, without challenging, drew his revolver and fired. A scream from his wife soon brought him the knowledge that he had shot his helpmate.

The revolver was a large "nevy" and carried a heavy ball. The ball struck the woman on the right shoulder and lodged in the body. A messenger was at once sent, and Dr. Heddens, of this city, was soon on hand. He dressed the wound and did all in his power to ease the pain consequent thereupon. The wound is a very dangerous one, but the attendant physician is satisfied that the lady will recover from its effects.

Mr. Moore is nigh frantic with grief at his sad mistake.

———•———

The Holt County Sentinel
OREGON, MISSOURI

JULY 2, 1869

Col. Wm. B. Mason, of Maricita, while on a visit to his brother-in-law in Adams township, Muskingum Co., on the 9th inst., accidentally shot his sister-in-law. The colonel had gone out to shoot a chicken, and seeing Mrs. Mason near the well, he went into the barn so that she would not be in range of his gun. Meantime the lady had passed around the barn, and was directly in range when the colonel fired. The ball passed through an inch board and struck Mrs. Mason in the bowels, about six inches above the groin. The ball has not been extracted. The physicians think the wound will not prove fatal.

The Coshocton Tribune
COSHOCTON, OHIO

❧

Yesterday morning, Mr. W. Squires, residing in Huntoon's addition, accidentally shot his little son, a boy three years old, causing his death in about an hour. It appears that Mr. S. had occasion to use his revolver, and went out of the house to fire it off. On returning, as he was entering the door, playing carelessly with the pistol in his hand, it suddenly went off. His little boy was standing at the time directly in front of him, and the ball struck him in the head, passing through the base of the brain, and coming out, struck Mrs. S., who was standing beside her son, inflicting a slight scratch upon her arm. Dr. Tefft was called in, and did everything in his power for the little sufferer, but without avail, as he died as stated above.

The Daily Kansas Tribune
LAWRENCE, KANSAS

❧

DISTRESSING—In Washington county, Kansas, Johnson Hammond accidentally shot his wife. While abed, his wife aroused him with the information that there were wolves about. Hammond rose, took his gun down from the joists above his head, and excitedly ran out carrying the gun in his left hand, butt toward the door. He ran about a half a mile, when he saw a wolf, and in raising his gun to take aim at it found it had been discharged. Returning to the house, he entered, and there stood four of his children crying, the eldest of whom said, "Papa, papa, mamma's dead." He, almost frantic, rushed to the bedside, and found his wife a corpse, her right breast pierced with a bullet. His infant, who had been sleeping beside the mother when he left the house, was caressing her dead body. It is supposed that when Hammond rushed out the door, the lock or trigger of the gun caught the jamb, and was discharged, the contents lodging in the breast of the deceased. Hammond swears he heard no report of the discharge of the gun. A coroner's jury acquitting him of all blame.

———◆———

The Indiana Weekly Messenger
INDIANA, PENNSYLVANIA

❖

MELANCHOLY ACCIDENT

At Salem, Marion county, Illinois, on Friday evening of last week, Miss P. M. Weldeson, a highly respected young lady, accidentally shot herself with a revolver, inflicting a mortal wound. The following are the circumstances:

Mr. Bohanan, of St. Louis, a young gentleman to whome she was to be married the following day, arrived at her home. At her request he opened his trunk to show her his wedding suit. He passed out several articles for inspection, and finally drew out a revolver, which she also wished to examine. While doing so, it was accidentally discharged, the ball entered between the ribs and ranging and downward, penetrated the stomach. She lingered in great anguish for a few hours, when she expired. Her affianced husband has been rendered practically insane by the sad occurrence, and is continually watched by friends, fearing that he will inflict personal injury upon himself.

Alton Telegraph
ALTON, ILLINOIS

MARCH 28, 1872

A tragedy most sad in its details took place in New York. William Trevert, a German citizen in comfortable circumstances, accidentally shot his wife with a pistol, killing her instantly. Trevert became a raving maniac when he saw what he had done.

Spirit of the Age
WOODSTOCK, VERMONT

MAY 24, 1872

Mr. Bland, of Dinwiddle county, Va., while examining an old gun, accidentally shot his little son and daughter, inflicting a painful wound in his son's shoulder, and several shot entering the face of his daughter, from which it is feared she will die.

The Raleigh News
RALEIGH, NORTH CAROLINA

❧

LOCAL JOTTINGS

. . . Onions are good for the epizootic.

. . . Are there to be any Christmas trees?

. . . We learn that the will of the late Frank Scott is to be contested.

. . . Alf Bailey fell down his cellar stairs yesterday bringing his face in contact with some hard substance. No bones broken, but it is reported that there is not a square inch of his face that is not bruised.

. . . The citizens of Decatur would give thanks to the City Council if some of the sidewalks in the city were repaired.

. . . We thought a good strong frost would put an end to shot–gun accidents, but people still blaze away at themselves.

———————

Decatur Weekly Republican
DECATUR, ILLINOIS

ACCIDENTAL SHOOTING

We record a melancholy accident with firearms last week, by which George Bentley of this place was accidentally wounded, and which may result in the loss of sight to one of his eyes. It appears that Bentley and Dickerson of San Francisco, and formerly of Woodland, went out hunting with dogs and guns, and while in the pursuit of quail along Cache Creek, Dickerson, having flushed a quail, fired at it in all haste, when Bentley happened to be in direct range of the gun and about thirty steps distant; the result was that the shot took effect in the face and neck of Bentley, one shot entering the nose near the eye, which produced total blindness, and up to his leaving for San Francisco on Monday no improvement was visible. He left on Monday morning for the purpose of consulting an oculist in the city, since which time we have heard nothing from him. The wounds inflicted by two or three other shots have occasioned him no great inconvenience.

Sacramento Daily Union
SACRAMENTO, CALIFORNIA

On Sunday in New York, Louis Rick, a butcher, of 453 West Forty-second street, cut his throat with a razor, and Ellen Bennis, aged twenty-five, accidentally shot herself at 193 West street.

The Kingston Daily Freeman
KINGSTON, NEW YORK

NOVEMBER 2, 1873

The Grass Valley Union contains an account of the death of William Stutridge, who accidentally shot his little son, on the 3d ult. It says that he slowly pined away from grief and remorse, and died of a broken heart. Typhoid fever set in at the last, and hastened his end.

Los Angeles Herald
LOS ANGELES, CALIFORNIA

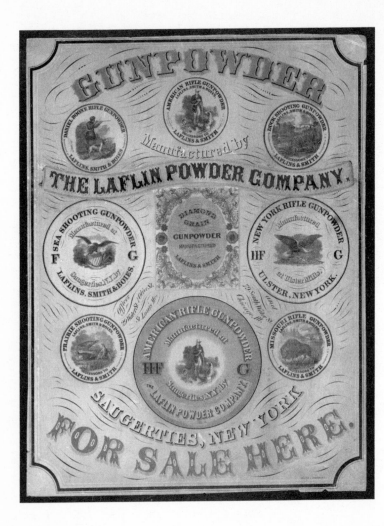

DECEMBER 17, 1873

❖

A dog accidentally shot his master at Bridgeport, Conn., lately.

———◆———

The Leavenworth Times
LEAVENWORTH, KANSAS

JANUARY 22, 1874

❊

A boy in Decatur, Ind., took a double-barrel gun a few days
ago to shoot a chicken, and three of his younger brothers
followed to see the fun. The boy shot the fowl—then threw
the gun with so much force upon the ground as to discharge
the other barrel, seriously wounding all the brothers—one
it is thought fatally.

The Eureka Herald
EUREKA, KANSAS

JUNE 22, 1874

※

A Kansas boy earned a nice Bible by committing three hundred verses to memory, and then he traded his Bible for a
shot-gun, and accidentally shot his aunt in the leg—a fearful warning to all aunts.

The Rutland Daily Globe
RUTLAND, VERMONT

❋

MELANCHOLY ACCIDENT
IN BROOKLYN

About 7 o'clock last evening, while Mr. Henry Bruckner, who had been out shooting on Long Island, was stepping from a Coney Island car at Fifteenth Street, near the city line, the hammer of his loaded gun caught in the guard of the seat and discharged the contents of the weapon into his left side. Mr. Bruckner fell forward on his face into the roadway, and died in a few minutes. The accident was witnessed by the wife and grandchildren of the unfortunate man, who had been spending the day at Coney Island, where he joined them at the conclusion of his day's sport. The remains were taken charge of by the Police of the Eighth Precinct and removed to the residence of the deceased. Mr. Bruckner was about fifty years of age.

The New York Times
NEW YORK, NEW YORK

❖

Henry Haynes, of Peoria, who accidentally shot his mother-in-law, has made three attempts to commit suicide. Some folks may sneer at him, but when one sits down and calmly reasons the thing, he must admit that it is hard to lose a mother-in-law just as the preserve season is at its height.

———

The Times–Picayune
New Orleans, Louisiana

◈

ACCIDENTS FROM FIREARMS

Several shot-gun accidents to report this week. Last Thursday, Marion Barngrover, of West Lincoln, while in his kitchen, dropped the breech of his gun on the floor, causing its discharge, and blowing off the thumb and fore finger of his right hand. A singular coincidence is that a few years ago, a man named Woodruff was injured in the same room by the accidental discharge of a gun. Two holes made in the ceiling by the two guns are not more than three feet apart.

Mr. Elijah Myers, while driving to town on Thursday, was struck in the face by a charge of shot fired at quails by someone at the roadside. One shot penetrated his eye, and he is in great danger of losing the sight in it.

Squire Emmitt, of Mt. Pulaski, was severely injured in one eye by the nipple of his gun being blown out of the barrel.

———➤———

The Pantagraph
BLOOMINGTON, ILLINOIS

❖❖

A few recent cases of accidental shootings are here re-corded: At Buffalo, N.Y., Miss Isabella P. Keene, a highly respectable young lady, went out to the barn to shoot rats with a pistol, and accidentally shot herself through the head. In the same city, Charles Broaker, while under the influ-ence of liquor, quarreled with his family, and threatened to shoot a policeman who was called. In the act of drawing his pistol, it went off, the ball passing into his bowels, inflicting a fatal wound. At Baltimore, Miss Lilly Stoy, 23 years old, was shot in the right leg, above the knee, while at a ball. The girl was dancing with a man at the time, when a pistol fell from his pocket, and went off. In Huntington County, Ind., Henry Uphile, an old man, and his son were engaged in try-ing to shoot a beef, when the boy accidentally discharged the contents of his gun into his father's stomach, inflicting a wound, from the effects of which the old man died. Near Middletown, Ohio, James Davis was unloading iron from a wagon. A piece of iron struck a revolver in his coat pocket, causing it to discharge. The ball pierced his heart, causing instant death. At West Liberty, Iowa, a son of Wm. S. Lane, 15 years old, in company with his sister, went to feed the hogs about a half-mile from his father's dwelling. He took a gun along for any game that chance might throw in his way. In reaching from the corn-crib down for the gun, the lock came in contact with the crib, causing the explosion, when the whole contents of the gun were discharged into the boy's brain, killing him almost instantly.

———◄►———

Eureka Herald
Eureka, Kansas

❧

FATAL ACCIDENT WITH
A REVOLVER

Julian Harrison, of the firm of Perkins & Harrison, a to-
bacco inspector and partner of the owners of the Shockoe
warehouse, accidentally shot himself today with an old
seven-shooter, which was kept in a drawer of a desk in his
office. He was looking through the drawer for something at
the time, and in moving the pistol out of the way it is supposed he struck the hammer, exploding the charge. The
ball entered his head, just above the bridge of the nose, going clear through and striking the ceiling of the room. He
fell back in a chair, and expired almost instantly.

The Weekly Star
WILMINGTON, NORTH CAROLINA

❖

FATAL ACCIDENT.—A very distressing and melancholy accident occurred in Perry county, near Sterrett's Gap, on Monday of last week. The particulars are that on Monday morning Mr. Frank Hoover took down his gun to clean and load it. The gun had no cap on it, nor was there a cap in the house. Mrs. Hoover was in the same room preparing a meal. After cleaning and loading the gun, Mr. Hoover rose to hang it in its place upon a joist when it exploded, the load entering his wife's body and inflicting a wound from which she died an hour thereafter. No reason can be given for the gun's explosion and the only conjecture thus far advanced is that in some way the fire from the stove communicated with the powder in the gun.

The Shippennsburg News
SHIPPENNSBURG, PENNSYLVANIA

❧

William Mellon, a resident of Henderson Street, Jersey City, met with a melancholy accident yesterday. He had gone with some friends to a resort on the Heights to shoot for game. While looking into the barrel of his gun the weapon went off and his head was literally blown off. He was married. The body was removed to the Morgue.

The New York Times
NEW YORK, NEW YORK

MELANCHOLY ACCIDENT

The residence of Mr. Robert Y. Hebden, No. 3902 Lake avenue, was the scene Christmas Day of a sad accident, the victim being Miss Kathleen Ada Hebden, a charming and cultured young lady, about 24 years old, who was visiting her brother. In the midst of Christmas pleasures, and during the temporary absence of her sister-in-law, she found a Smith & Wesson revolver in a drawer in the sideboard. It belonged to her brother, and was used by him in killing cats, and also regarded as a handy weapon in case of such unwelcome visitors as burglars. Miss Hebden, in handling the piece, accidentally touched the trigger and exploded a cartridge, the bullet entering the left breast, killing her instantly, and, emerging, entered the wood work of a mirror.

The report brought the inmates of the house immediately to the scene, but life was extinct. Miss Hebden was born in Hamilton, Canada, where her father was rector of the Episcopal Church. The Coroner held an inquest on the remains of the unfortunate lady yesterday, and the theory of suicide being exploded by the evidence, a verdict was returned of death by bullet accidentally fired from the revolver. There was no evidence of melancholy, nor could the slightest cause be found for a self-murder; on the contrary, everything pointed to a sad accident, the result of probable carelessness engendered by a familiar acquaintance with pistols, and Miss Hebden was regarded as an expert shot.

————◆————

The Inter Ocean
CHICAGO, ILLINOIS

❖

A FATAL SHOT

THE MELANCHOLY ACCIDENT
WHICH OVERTOOK
A FOURTEEN YEAR OLD BOY

A Singular fatality appears to be following the boys of late. Within the past two weeks no less than six accidents have occurred wherein boys ranging in age from eight to fourteen years have been the victims. One was killed outright, another was said to be mortally wounded and the others received more or less dangerous gunshot wounds.

Yesterday a most distressing accident occurred at No. 74 St. Anthony, between Morales and Urquhart streets, which resulted in the almost instant death of George Hanff, a boy 14 years of age, who was playing with a toy pistol loaded with ball cartridge. It was about four o'clock in the afternoon, and George was in the backyard of his mother's premises. An ax was lying in the yard, and the machinery of the pistol becoming deranged in some manner the boy sought to remedy the defect.

He struck the pistol several blows against the ax, when he unfortunately struck the hammer of the weapon against the implement, causing the cartridge to explode. The bullet took effect in the right side of the poor boy's breast, just above the nipple, and he fell forward and expired a few moments afterward.

Coroner LeMonnier was immediately notified and held an inquest, returning a verdict of accidental death from a gunshot wound of the right breast.

———•———

The Daily Picayune
New Orleans, Louisiana

❖

SHOT BY ACCIDENT

A serious accident occurred here today. Mrs. James Dyer, a middle-aged lady, was accidentally shot. Her son, aged about 17, had his gun loaded and on his shoulder. A dog belonging to the family was playing with him, by jumping up on him. The dog knocked the gun from the boy's shoulder, and falling, it was discharged, the load striking her left leg below the knee, breaking the bones so badly that amputation was necessary.

The Courier Journal
LOUISVILLE, KENTUCKY

❈

ACCIDENTALLY KILLED

A YOUNG WOMAN EXPERT WITH FIREARMS SHOOTS HERSELF

PHILADELPHIA—Miss Annie C., daughter of Mrs. James Lesley, of this city, recently went to visit the family of Mr. Wm. H. Nichols, of Brooklyn. Miss Lesley was unusually fond of outdoor sports, and had won quite a reputation for skill in such as a lady could with propriety engage. She was noted as a player of lawn tennis, and was especially skillful in the use of firearms. During a sojourn in the Adirondacks she brought down a deer with her unerring rifle, a feat so rarely performed by a lady that its successful achievement rendered Miss Lesley quite a heroine throughout that mountain region.

With Mr. George Nichols, a son of her host, Miss Lesley had been in the habit of practicing frequently with the pistol during a summer recently spent at Saratoga. While visiting at his father's house, she resumed her pistol practice, with young Mr. Nichol's assistance, and was so engaged on Saturday afternoon, when the melancholy accident occurred which, in an instant, deprived her of her life. The pistol she was handling went off suddenly, lodging a bullet in her brain, and her horror-stricken companion beheld her sink at his feet in the agonies of death. The body reached the city this evening.

———◆———

National Republican
WASHINGTON, D.C.

LOST CREEK—Troublesome Creek seems to be unlucky for deputy sheriffs. On the 28th of May, 1887, Deputy Sheriff J. S. Park, of Breathirt county, accidentally shot himself in the leg on Caney, a tributary to Troublesome, and today, at the mouth of Russell's Branch about two miles below Caney on Troublesome, Red Sam Napier, deputy sheriff of Perry county, on his return from taking a man by the name of Cody to the penitentiary, accidentally shot his horse through the neck, which fell on Napier smashing his big jug and came very near breaking his leg.

The Hazel Green Herald
HAZEL GREEN, KENTUCKY

NOVEMBER 12, 1888

❦

Horry Paramore has suffered a severe loss. While hunting on Saturday he accidentally shot his dog dead. He was a fine animal, the friend of everybody, and is a heavy money loss.

———◆———

The Ottawa Daily Republic
OTTAWA, KANSAS

A TWELVE-YEAR OLD BOY ACCIDENTALLY SHOOTS HIS MOTHER

ASHEVILLE, N.C.—News has just reached this place of a horrible accident near Hot Springs, Madison county. A twelve-year old son of S. D. Chambers, a highly respected farmer, accidentally shot and instantly killed his mother. The father had been to Hot Springs, bringing home with him a valise with some articles for the family in it. He put the valise down in the house and stepped out. When the lad looked into it to see what his father had brought him, he found a pistol, and said to his mother, "See what pa brought home." The pistol was discharged, the ball striking his mother in the breast. Her only words were: "Oh, Lord, you have killed me."

The People's Press
WINSTON-SALEM, NORTH CAROLINA

❖

A MELANCHOLY ACCIDENT

PORTLAND, ME. April 23. This afternoon at Deering Point, Robert Hamilton, aged 16, employed at the Preble House as an elevator boy, while playing with a revolver accidentally discharged it without knowing that his half-brother, Perley Offen, aged 12, was in range. The bullet entered Perley's temple, killing him instantly. The shooting was purely accidental.

Boston Daily Journal
BOSTON, MASSACHUSETTS

❖

SHOT BY A FRIEND

A PROMINENT DEMOCRAT SEVERELY WOUNDED BY A REPUBLICAN

CHARLESTON, W. VA.—A dangerous case of accidentally shooting occurred on the streets here last night. Squire A. J. Hammock, a prominent Republican of this county, was talking on the street last night with Hon. C. P. Synder, the Democratic candidate for Judge of the Criminal Court of the county. For some unknown reason Hammock drew his revolver from his pocket, when it exploded, the ball passing through his hand and into Snyder just below the abdomen, striking the pubic bone.

The ball cannot be located on account of the swelling, and the wound may prove dangerous. Both parties unite in saying the shooting was entirely accidental.

———◆———

The Pittsburg Dispatch
PITTSBURGH, PENNSYLVANIA

Melancholy Accident—J. D. Crimmins, Jr., of New York, while gunning for birds on his father's country seat at Noroton, Connecticut, last week, stumbled on a rock and his gun was accidently discharged, young Crimmins receiving the charge in his face. The sight of his right eye was entirely destroyed.

Irish World
NEW YORK, NEW YORK

❖

MISTAKEN FOR A BURGLAR

A YOUNG MAN SHOT BY HIS BROTHER IN LAW BY ACCIDENT

WHEELING, W. VA.—George Hess of Fulton was mistaken for a burglar by his two brothers in law, named Ball, at Pleasant Valley, yesterday morning and shot, dying instantly. Mrs. Hess had been in delicate health, and her husband fearing the flood decided to take his family to the residence of his mother in law, at Pleasant Valley. The party did not arrive at the Ball residence until after midnight and Mr. Hess tried to get around the sleeping family. With his little child in his arms he went upon the porch and called several times. The two young men of the family saw the form on the porch and thinking there was to be a repetition of the attempt to enter made by burglars last Sunday night, armed themselves and went to the door. When they opened it Mr. Hess spoke and attempted to enter. Ezekiel, the younger brother, fired, and Hess, still clasping his child, fell to the porch dead. The child screamed, "Oh, papa is dead," and the boys ran out and discovered what they had done. The young man at once came to the city and gave himself up. There was a verdict of accidental shooting.

———•———

New-York Tribune
NEW YORK, NEW YORK

❈

A MELANCHOLY ACCIDENT

LEAVE ASKED TO INCREASE DAMAGES CLAIMED

A melancholy accident, which occurred on Beacon Hill nearly ten years ago, and resulted in the total blindness of a bright boy of 12 years, was recalled in the Fifth Session of the Superior Court this morning on a motion made in a suit in which damages are claimed for the injury sustained. In the fall of 1881, Augustus N. Loring and William Amory, the latter a son of Charles W. Amory, and both residents of Beacon Street, were playing together near their homes. The Amory boy had a toy pistol in his hand, and in some way, it is alleged, the pistol exploded and the contents of the barrel entered the eye of the Loring boy, who not only lost the sight of that eye but also in a few weeks became totally blind, the other eye having become affected in consequence of the shock. The matter was put by the Loring boy's parents into the hands of A. A. Ranney, and he brought a suit in 1881 against the Amory boy to recover damages placed at $20,000, and another against the boy's father for $30,000. It is understood the latter has been discontinued. In court today Fletcher Ranney, counsel for the Lorings, asked for leave to increase the damages claimed from $20,000 to $40,000. Lawyer Dabney, for the defendant, opposed the motion. He said the case grew out of a deplorable accident, which had been a blight on the life of the defendant, who had done everything that he could for the plaintiff since its occurrence.

Boston Daily Journal
BOSTON, MASSACHUSETTS

❧

BLEW HIS HEAD OFF

ACCIDENTAL SHOOTING AFFRAY IN A HUNTING PARTY

MITCHELL, S.D., NOV 20.—Banker Thomas A. Short of Edgerton met a horrible death early this morning. In company with a party of friends he went to the Missouri River. A good hunting party had secreted themselves awaiting early morning flight of birds from the river to their feeding grounds. Upon approach of a flock to within shooting distance Charles Rebee raised his gun and at the same instant another man who was five or six feet in advance suddenly rose to his feet receiving the entire charge of buck shot from Rebee's gun in the head, blowing it all to pieces.

Grand Forks Daily Herald
GRAND FORKS, NORTH DAKOTA

❖

ACCIDENTALLY SHOT HER SON

HARTFORD, CONN.—Mrs. Sanders, of New Britain, accidentally shot her son Edward, 15 years old. He was keeping a revolver for a playmate, and his mother did not intend to let him carry it. He showed her how harmless it was, and then she took it and pulled the trigger. The ball entered the boy's chest, passed through the right lung, and lodged in the muscles of the back. He cannot recover.

———◆———

Harrisburg Daily Independent
HARRISBURG, PENNSYLVANIA

❈

ACCIDENTALLY SHOT A WOMAN

Mrs. J. Plum, living southeast of Iowa Falls, was accidentally shot. Her son was up stairs cleaning his shotgun, which was accidentally discharged, the load passing through the floor and entering Mrs. Plum's shoulder and side. The accident may not result fatally, but the loss of the wounded arm may possibly result.

———◆———

The Alden Times
ALDEN, IOWA

❖

A BULLET

FROM A FATHER'S PISTOL
PASSES THROUGH
THE HEAD OF HIS DAUGHTER

BROWNSVILLE, TENN.—One of the most horrible accidents in the history of Brownsville happened here this morning. Deputy Sheriff R. R. Grove accidentally shot his daughter, Miss Susie, through the head with a .38 caliber pistol. The ball entered the center of the eye, and passed entirely through the head. Grove was sitting on his portico cleaning his pistol, while his daughter was coming up the walk from the front gate. Just as she reached the steps the pistol was discharged, with the above result. The young lady is alive, but there is no chance for recovery. She is 24 years old, and a universal favorite. The father is crazed with grief.

The Cincinnati Enquirer
CINCINNATI, OHIO

❖

A TRIP INTO MAINE

It is claimed for this state that it has running wild in its woods more deer than there are in the other five New England States, with all the Middle States included. With her well stocked streams and ponds and lakes and the moose and caribou, the latter being protected by law from being hunted, Maine is now the chief resort for hunting game in the northeast section of our country. Here no dogging is permitted of deer or moose, and the hunter, relying on his own woodcraft, is obliged to pit it against the shyness, alertness, and instincts of self-preservation of the game he is in quest of. Hunting is excellent here, deer tracks and their runaways being seen in all the woods.

The recent shooting of Mr. Dumond of Boston by his guide adds another to the list of these melancholy accidents of mistaking him for a deer. The frequency of these fatal occurrences calls for some concert of action on the part of the guides of this state as well as that of the sportsmen who come here in search of big game. If such sad mistakes are due, as it is claimed by some, to criminal negligence, who is going to define negligence? If an experienced guide, like the one who killed Mr. Dumond, makes such a fatal error, what is to be expected of those who are amateur hunters in the excitement of the hunt? At least one step might be taken to make such unfortunate accidents less likely and that is to have the hunting fraternity adopt, as far as circumstances will permit, some uniformity of color in its hunting dress.

———•———

The Brooklyn Eagle
BROOKLYN, NEW YORK

❖

HARRY REYNOLDS SHOT DEAD

BULLET FROM A RIFLE THAT HIS BROTHER DROPS PIERCES HIS HEART

Harry V. Reynolds, 11 years old, was accidentally shot and killed by his brother, George Reynolds, 13 years old, in the parlor of the Reynolds home, at No. 136 Lund avenue, Rogers Park. George had been hunting ducks and had returned home about 10 o'clock in the morning. His younger brother was sitting on a lounge reading a book which had been presented to him as a New Year's gift.

George was holding his rifle in his hand and telling what success he had in his hunting trip, when the weapon suddenly fell to the floor and was discharged. It was a thirty-two-caliber rifle, and the ball pierced the base of Henry's heart and killed him instantly. The noise of the shot attracted the attention of the family, and they hurriedly came to the parlor, where they found the older brother attempting in vain to stop the flow of blood. He had his handkerchief in his hand and was doing his best to relieve the sufferer. A physician was sent for, but before he arrived the boy was dead.

The grief of the brother who had fired the fatal shot knew no bounds. He wept and moaned and declared that he wanted to kill himself too. When the police arrived he begged to be taken to the station, and told Lieutenant No-elle that he should lock him up in the cell. The boy was permitted to go home, as the shooting was accidental. The coroner will hold the inquest today.

———————

The Inter Ocean
CHICAGO, ILLINOIS

❖

UNFORTUNATE AND FATAL ACCIDENT

A few days before Christmas Mr. M. H. Underdunk, agent of the Norfolk and Western Railway Company at Pounding Mill, in this county, was accidentally shot by a Westchester rifle in the hands of Conductor Rice Irvin, and died on Christmas day from the wound. Mr. Underdunk had handed the rifle to Mr. Irvin to examine, and when the latter undertook to hand the gun back to Mr. Underdunk the trigger in some way hung in Irvin's clothing, the gun was discharged and shot Underdunk in the knee. After several days the attending physicians found it necessary to amputate the injured leg, hoping that the operation would save the unfortunate man's life; but the effort was unavailing, and he died as before stated on Christmas day.

The deceased was an excellent gentleman and faithful employee of the railway company. At one time he was assistant agent at Tazewell, and was highly esteemed by all who knew him here. About six months ago he was married to Miss

Mollie McGraw, who was a student at Tazewell College last year.

It was a very unfortunate accident, and ought to teach persons the great danger of handling firearms carelessly.

———•———

Tazewell Republican
TAZEWELL, VIRGINIA

ACCIDENTAL KILLING.

Jesse McIntosh was accidentally shot and killed by his son-in-law, James Harrison, on Caloway's creek Christmas day. The particulars as we learned are about as follows: Sam Walden had prepared a Christmas dinner and McIntosh was present. He and Walden became engaged in a quarrel over politics and started together for a scrap when Henry Alcorn took hold of McIntosh to prevent trouble and Harrison wrenched a pistol from Walden's hand. By this time McIntosh had released himself from Alcorn and was coming on to Walden again. Harrison was pleading with him and motioning for him to stay back with the pistol in his hand which was cocked when he got it from Walden. It went off and the ball struck McIntosh just above the heart killing him instantly. He was buried Wednesday under the auspices of the Masonic fraternity, he being a member of the Lodge at this place. He leaves a wife and several small children, and two married daughters.

The Spout Spring Times
SPOUT SPRINGS, KENTUCKY

❖

ACCIDENTALLY SHOT.

CHRISTMAS FESTIVITIES
AT THE HOME OF JOHN BUECHTEL
COME TO A SUDDEN END

LOUISVILLE, KY., DEC. 26—A fatal accident put a sudden end to the Christmas festivities at the home of John Buechel, on Sixteenth street near Grayson, Sunday evening. Jacob F. Huntow, Buechel's brother-in-law, with the former's wife and four children, were among the merrymakers. Huntow played the part of Santa Claus, and in his outfit carried a revolver. While the frolic was at its height this weapon was accidentally discharged, the bullet striking and instantly killing Mrs. Huntow. When he realized what had happened, Huntow threatened to take his life, and became so violent that the police thought best to lock him up.

Crittenden Press
MARION, KENTUCKY

❖

GOD REMOVES A BULLET IN HIS OWN WAY.

From a letter written by D. W. Lehning, of the firm of Kelly, Stiger & Co., Omaho, Nebraska, we quote:

I desire to testify to God's goodness to me in preserving my life from destruction, as the result of a bullet fired from the revolver of some careless person trying to demonstrate his Fourth of July patriotism.

On May 19, 1899, God removed a .38-caliber bullet, without the aid of a knife or loss of one drop of blood, and without even a suggestion of pain, after it had been embedded in my hand for nearly nine months.

Leaves of Healing
CHICAGO, ILLINOIS

❧

BOY ACCIDENTALLY SHOT.

WILLIE KERN RECEIVES A LOAD OF NO. 4 SHOT IN THE BOWELS AND WILL PROBABLY DIE.

Willie Kern, 13 years old, son of Adolph Kern, a farmer living four miles south of the city, was accidentally shot yesterday afternoon at 1 o'clock and there is thought to be but little hope for his recovery. He received the contents of a heavily loaded gun in the bowels and groin, badly tearing the ligaments and lacerating the flesh.

The accident occurred about one-half mile from the boy's home. Yesterday afternoon the lad, calling his dog, shouldered a gun and with a companion named King, about the same age and the son of an adjoining farmer, went out for a hunt. The boy kept the gun cocked all the while and about 1 o'clock he leaned the weapon up against a large stone and went in front of the muzzle for some purpose. While he was in this position the dog knocked the gun off the stone and it discharged. A cry of pain followed the sharp report of the gun and little Willie threw up his hands, cried "I'm shot" and fell unconscious to the ground. The contents of the gun, which was heavily loaded with No. 4 shot, struck him while he was facing the weapon and his bowels and groin were almost perforated. The ugly wound bled profusely and his companion ran to the house leaving the boy to wallow in his blood.

Dr. Roberts was despatched for and he went out at 1:30. When he arrived the boy had been removed to his home and was in a dangerous condition. The wounds were temporarily dressed and everything possible done to save the lad's life, but there seems but little chance for him to survive the terrible accident. Dr. Roberts made no attempt to extract the shot as they were imbedded deeply in the stomach and bowels.

The boy will probabaly be brought to Mercy hospital.

———◆———

Fort Scott Daily Monitor
FORT SCOTT, KANSAS

❖

ACCIDENTALLY SHOT HIS SISTER.

BETHLEHEM, PA., JAN. 7.—Harry Delp, the 13-year-old son of Frank Delp, a wealthy farmer of Lower Saucon, to-day accidentally shot and fatally wounded his 10-year-old sister. Harry while his parents were absent found his father's loaded revolver and while his sister was looking into the barrel it was discharged. The bullet entered the left side of the little girl's forehead. The lad bandaged the wound as best he could and hurried with his sister to the hospital here. The doctors say she cannot recover.

The Wilkes-Barre Record
WILKES-BARRE, PENNSYLVANIA

❦

ACCIDENTAL SHOT ENDS HER LIFE

MRS. COTTON FALLS WITH BULLET IN HER HEART WHILE PUTTING PISTOL INTO A TRUNK.

OAKLAND, MARCH 2.—Mrs. Edna Cotton, wife of Colonel W. J. Cotton, accidentally shot herself through the heart with a revolver this afternoon at the Hotel Metropole while preparing to attend a dinner to be given by her husband at the Athenian Club. Death was almost instantaneous. The shooting took place a few minutes before 5 o'clock. Colonel Cotton was then at the Athenian Club making the final arrangements for the affair to be given by him.

Mrs. Cotton was in their apartments at the hotel preparing to dress for the evening. With her was Miss Mabel Hall, who was to accompany her to the dinner party. On a table in the front room of the suit was lying Colonel Cotton's revolver. Mrs. Cotton took up the weapon to lay it away. While she was placing it in a trunk in the bedroom the weapon was discharged, and Mrs. Cotton dropped dead on the floor between the trunk and the bed.

Miss Hall turned as she heard the report of the pistol and saw Mrs. Cotton fall. She ran into the hallway and screamed for assistance. The bellboys responded and Drs. Kitchens and Green, who were in the hotel, were called. After a hasty examination they pronounced the woman dead. Word was telephoned to the husband at the Athenian Club to the effect that his wife had fainted. He immediately started for the hotel, taking Dr. Medros with him. When he arrived the sad news was broken to him.

Miss Hall, in speaking of the accident, said: "I was in the rooms with Mrs. Cotton. We were preparing to attend the supper to be given by Colonel Cotton. Mrs. Cotton had laid her dress out when she noticed the pistol lying on a table in the front room. She said she thought she had better lay the weapon away. I asked her not to touch it. She laughed and said she had handled it before and was not afraid of it. She picked the weapon up and went into the bedroom. The next thing I heard was the report of the weapon. I turned and saw Mrs. Cotton fall. I then ran into the hall and called for help."

No one knows exactly how the weapon came to be discharged. It is supposed that the trigger caught on something as Mrs. Cotton was about to place it in the trunk. Colonel Cotton is distracted with grief and refuses to be seen. He and his wife returned from San Jose about ten days ago. He is proprietor of the Mobile Agency in this city and at San Jose. He and his wife had been married twelve years. They resided formerly in Arizona. There are two young sons, who are now at San Jose.

———◆———

San Francisco Chronicle
SAN FRANCISCO, CALIFORNIA

HARPER'S WEEKLY.

A JOURNAL OF CIVILIZATION

Vol. XXIII.—No. 1190.] NEW YORK, SATURDAY, OCTOBER 18, 1879. [PRICE TEN CENTS.

Entered according to Act of Congress, in the Year 1879, by Harper & Brothers, in the office of the Librarian of Congress at Washington.

DEATH AT THE POLLS, AND FREE FROM "FEDERAL INTERFERENCE."

WAS ACCIDENTALLY SHOT.

THE YOUNG MOTHER WAS PREPARING HER BABY FOR A BATH.

LOUISVILLE, KY., FEB. 26.—While preparing a bath for her 15-months-old baby Mrs. Emma Brock, aged 19, accidentally killed herself Sunday evening. In opening a dresser drawer to get the infant's clothes the string on one of the garments caught on the trigged of a pistol in the drawer, causing the weapon to be discharged. The bullet passed through Mrs. Brock's heart. She lived long enough to say to her husband, Harry Brock, who was lying on a bed: "I am shot." The Brock house is at 120 Shelby street.

Mount Vernon Signal
MOUNT VERNON, KENTUCKY

❧

MESSENGER BOY
ACCIDENTALLY SHOT.

DEATH COMES TO SEVENTEEN-YEAR OLD
WILLIAM McKEE AT VINCENNES, IND.

VINCENNES, IND., FEB. 28.—[Special]—William McKee, 17 years old, whose father is supposed to live in Terre Haute, fatally shot himself to-night. The ball entered over the heart. Nobody saw the shooting.

McKee remained conscious long enough to say that the shooting was accidental, and requested that his aunt, Mrs. Lizzie Adamson, of Bruceville, be notified. McKee was a Western Union messenger and last week asked the police for permission to carry a revolver, which was refused.

The Courier-Journal
LOUISVILLE, KENTUCKY

❦

RESIGNED FROM CONSTABULARY

TROOPER CARLTON BROKEN IN HEALTH BECAUSE OF HAVING ACCIDENTALLY SHOT COMRADE.

Frederick M. Carlton, the State trooper who accidentally shot trooper John Garscia and which accident resulted in the latter's death, has resigned from the constabulary and has gone to New York, where he is to assume another position.

His resignation is due to his being deeply affected over the shooting. Since the accident he has lost his appetite and his health failed, and he was unable to get the matter out of his thoughts. The other members of the troop feared that he would lose his mind and a careful watch was kept. It is feared that Carlton may find it necessary to enter a sanitarium.

The Wilkes-Barre Record
WILKES-BARRE, PENNSYLVANIA

❖

FATHER AND SON SHOT
BY SAME GUN

STOCKBRIDGE, MICH., APRIL 1.—Accidentally shot by the same gun that killed his 12-year-old son, Purdy, about two weeks ago, E. Smith, a farmer, five miles northeast of here, died tonight.

The boy was fatally wounded on a hunting trip while visiting relatives by the accidental discharge of his gun and died a few days later. Today, Smith started to pull the same gun from his buggy where it had lain since the accident to his son when the weapon was discharged, the shot tearing a hole in his right side and exposing the lung. At last report Smith was still alive but it is thought he cannot survive.

———◆———

Detroit Free Press
DETROIT, MICHIGAN

❖

BOY KILLS SISTER.

With the words, "Look out or I will shoot you," it is alleged Ernest Raeger, aged 15, accidentally shot and killed his sister, Caroline Raeger, aged 19, at their home in Westmoreland City, near Greensburg, last week. The boy with two friends, Rudolph Steck, aged 18, and Luke Pierce, aged 20, had gone to the rear of the house to shoot with a .22 calibre rifle. The young woman went out to the yard to see what the boys were shooting and was turning to go back to the house when her brother said jestingly "Look out or I will shoot you" and without aiming the gun, pulled the trigger. The girl fell with a bullet in her heart.

———✦———

Indiana Weekly Messenger
INDIANA, PENNSYLVANIA

❦

"BOY WHO FIRED SHOT IN SERIOUS CONDITION."

RAYMOND LITZENBERGER IN IGNORANCE OF PLAYMATE'S DEATH.

Raymond Litzenberger, the boy who last week accidentally shot Donald Smoyer, son of Mr. and Mrs. Oliver Smoyer of near East Texas, is in a very critical condition at his home. The Smoyer boy died at the hospital on Tuesday night as a result of the shooting and it is feared that when young Litzenberger learns that shot terminated fatally it will kill him. He is at the home of his parents, Mr. and Mrs. Irwin Litzenberger at East Texas and his condition is such that the attending physician has given instructions that he shall not under any circumstances be informed of his playmate's death.

Litzenberger is only thirteen years of age. The boys had been playmates since they were babies.

When the shooting occurred young Litzenberger fainted and it was hours before he recovered consciousness, several physicians being called to attend him.

———◆———

The Allentown Leader
ALLENTOWN, PENNSYLVANIA

❖

CHRISTMAS RIFLE DEADLY

GIRL ACCIDENTALLY SHOT ON NEW YEAR'S EVE DIES.

TARRYTOWN, N.Y., JAN. 3.—Accidentally wounded by a bullet from an air rifle, Dorothy Madden, the fifteen-year-old daughter of Mrs. Harry Madden, of Pocantico Hills, died in the Tarrytown hospital.

The girl was attending a New Year's party at the home of her uncle, Phillip Madden, in Hudson Terrace. About half an hour after midnight she was sitting on a sofa with George Sinnot, a boy of her own age, who was showing her an air rifle he had received as a Christmas present. In some way the spring was released while the muzzle pointed at her, and a bullet struck her in the forehead.

The News
FREDERICK, MARYLAND

꩜

CHILD ACCIDENTALLY SHOT.

SPECIAL DISPATCH TO THE ENQUIRER.

ZANESVILLE, OHIO, JANUARY 2.—Alice Newell, 5 years old, of Rockcut, eight miles north of the city, was fatally shot to-day. She and a little dog were the only ones in a room, and it is supposed that the dog knocked over a loaded shot-gun. The shot pierced the little girl's abdomen. The Newall child died to-night at 8 o'clock.

The Cincinnati Enquirer
CINCINNATI, OHIO

BABY ACCIDENTALLY SHOT BY SISTER

SNAPPED TRIGGER OF RIFLE ON BED WHERE CHILD WAS LYING AND BULLET PASSES THROUGH ITS BODY.

SPECIAL TO THE CAPITAL.

BURLINGTON, KAN., FEB. 1.—Harry, the 10-months-old baby of Mr. and Mrs. Albert Martindale, who live in the Center Valley neighborhood near Waverly, this county, was shot and killed a few days ago by a gun that was thought to be empty. James, a brother of the baby, who is 12 years old, laid a rifle on a bed where the infant was, and a sister, aged 9, snapped the trigger. The ball penetrated the stomach of the baby and ranged upwards. It emerged near the shoulder and embedded itself in the wall of the room.

The child lived a few hours and congestion of the lungs, where the ball passed through, caused its death.

The Topeka Daily Capital
TOPEKA, KANSAS

❖

KEPT ON IRONING.

NEW YORK.—Accidentally shot in the knee by her eleven-year-old nephew who was playing with a revolver, Mrs. Lillian M. Thomas continued to iron handkerchiefs. Her task finished, she notified a physician.

The Red Cloud Chief
RED CLOUD, NEBRASKA

❧

ONE MORE CASE OF "DIDN'T KNOW IT WAS LOADED."

FAXON.—Hazel Jennings, 7-year-old daughter of Mr. and Mrs. C. E. Jennings, accidentally shot and killed her 8-year-old brother, Richard. The Jennings family lives on a farm about one mile west of Faxon.

The little girl picked up a target rifle in the corner of a room where the rifle had been placed by an elder brother who had just returned from a hunt. She did not know that the rifle was loaded. She pointed the weapon toward her little brother and pulled the trigger. The .22 caliber bullet pierced the little boy's right eye and passed through his head, causing instant death. The Jennings family is well known in Comanche county, having lived here since the opening of the country to settlement.

———◆———

The Democrat-American
SALLISAW, OKLAHOMA

ILLUSTRATION CREDITS

Grateful acknowledgment is made to the following for permission to reprint their illustrations:

ii–iii Courtesy of San Francisco History Center, San Francisco Public Library

viii Courtesy of Music Division, Library of Congress

37 Courtesy of Rare Book and Special Collections Division, Library of Congress LC-USZ62-31149

62 Courtesy of Wellcome Trust

83 Courtesy of San Francisco History Center, San Francisco Public Library

99 Courtesy of Prints and Photographs Division, Library of Congress LC-USZ62-102738

104 Courtesy of San Francisco History Center, San Francisco Public Library

119 Courtesy of Rare Book and Special Collections Division, Library of Congress LC-USZ62-31793

140 Courtesy of Prints and Photographs Division, Library of Congress LC-DIG-pga-04180

188 Courtesy of Prints and Photographs Division, Library of Congress LC-USZ62-127750

204–205 From the Lincoln Financial Foundation Collection, courtesy of the Allen County Public Library and Indiana State Museum

ABOUT THE AUTHOR

PETER MANSEAU is a fellow at the Smithsonian Institution. He is the author of *Rag and Bone*, *Songs for the Butcher's Daughter*, *Vows*, and *One Nation, Under Gods*. He is the winner of the National Jewish Book Award, the American Library Association's Sophie Brody Medal, the Ribalow Prize for Fiction, and a National Endowment for the Arts Literature Fellowship. A founding editor of *Killing the Buddha*, he lives in Annapolis, Maryland.

beyond, where their surging forms are seen ... circling on the beach, the billows of old ocean dance along ... e shore, tossing the spray from their snowy crests high ... to the air.

It is a spectacle truly grand. Camps Wool ... and Winfield, as well as the Rhode Island Battery, whose ... sheltered horses and men were only yesterday put down ... the beach, must have suffered fearfully.

General Burnside, who thus far has maintained his ac- ... astomed cheerfulness and resolution under all this load ... responsibility, watches the careering storm from the ... ck of the *Admiral*, and seems weighed down with the ... cumulating misfortunes. His whole concern is for these ... mes. Occasionally he is heard to exclaim, in suppressed ... ny, "This is terrible!" "What will they do?" No one will ... The poor men, what will they do?" Nor a Moses, ... at such a man is beloved by the men, "Be still." Nor a Moses, ... insign'y, to say to the winds, "Be still." Nor a Moses, ... th power to smite the rock, and bid the waters to gush ... rth to supply their wants. They must wait on Provi- ... ence, whose ways are past finding out, and who, "doeth ... l things well." "The General says he rests in the assur- ... ce that same wise purpose will be accomplished by these ... range adversities. We are, he says, as so many grains ... sand in the hands of the Almighty. The condition of ... nor at the siege of Louisburg, seem only fitting parallels ... his situation. Yet he seems as strong-hearted as on the ... ador led to one despair of the result. The heavens are ... ly overcast.

The largest of the pictures on page 101 repre- ... ents Fort Hatteras, with Fort Clarke in the dis- ... ance. We illustrated the spot very fully at the ... me General Butler first occupied it. The view ... ow given is taken from the inlet. At high-water ... he fort is an island, and the troops travel to the ... un shown in the fore-ground of our picture on a ... lank-bridge resting on barrels. The stakes on ... he left of the picture mark the graves of soldiers; ... he building on the right is devoted to the conden- ... g of water by the aid of patent condensers. Cap- ... in Morris, of the First Artillery, is in command ... f the post.

One of the designs at the top of the page shows ... s the steamer *George L. Peabody* unshipping the ... orses of the Rhode Island Artillery, at Fort Hat- ... ras. Another presents a view of the steamer ... ure sinking in Hatteras Inlet on 14th January; ... d also of the steamer *New York* on the bar with ...